Harmonics for ukulele

Examples of practical use and songbook

Ondřej Šárek

Contents

ISBN-13: 978-1502949578
ISBN-10: 1502949571

Introduction

Harmonics or Flageolett is also widespread technique for stringed instruments. Due to the harmonics the range of the instrument extends. Therefore, it is good to be able to play.

The most basic division is the natural harmonics and artificial harmonics, from which we will build in the book.

Natural harmonics can be described. The left hand touches the string above the fret (do not press the string to the fretboard!) and the right hand strike. Natural harmonics can be used, but only on certain frets (4, 5, 7, 9, 12, 19).

In contrast, artificial harmonics can be described that the left hand holds a certain touch on a string. The index finger of the right hand lightly touches over 12 (or 7 or 5) the same fret the strings and the thumb or ring finger of the right hand strike the string.

Simultaneously we apply in harmonics, the higher the tone , the harder it is to play . It depends a lot on the ukulele , the strings , the hit place on the strings . From my experience , I better play harmonics on larger ukulele, by longer nails (or a plectrum when it is allowed by the song arrangement.)

How to read tablature

Natural harmonic: The left hand is placed lightly (do not press the string to the fretboard!) over a 12th fret of C strings and the right hand plays the string C.

Artificial harmonic: Stay on the first fret on the E string with your left hand. The index finger of the right hand put lightly over 13th fret (do not press the string to the fretboard!) and play the string E with a thumb or a ring finger.

At the beginning of the book there is a table of natural and artificial harmonics. You can play higher harmonics, but worse and it is not certain whether they'll be sounded .

After the table spread follows where you will find examples of the most commonly used chords using only natural harmonics.

The other six sites show major and minor arpeggios with artificial harmonics. It's good exercise for the next play. Play slowly at first , and note that the highest notes may not sound right , there is a need to practice.

Score

Natural and Artificial Harmonics

Ondřej Šárek

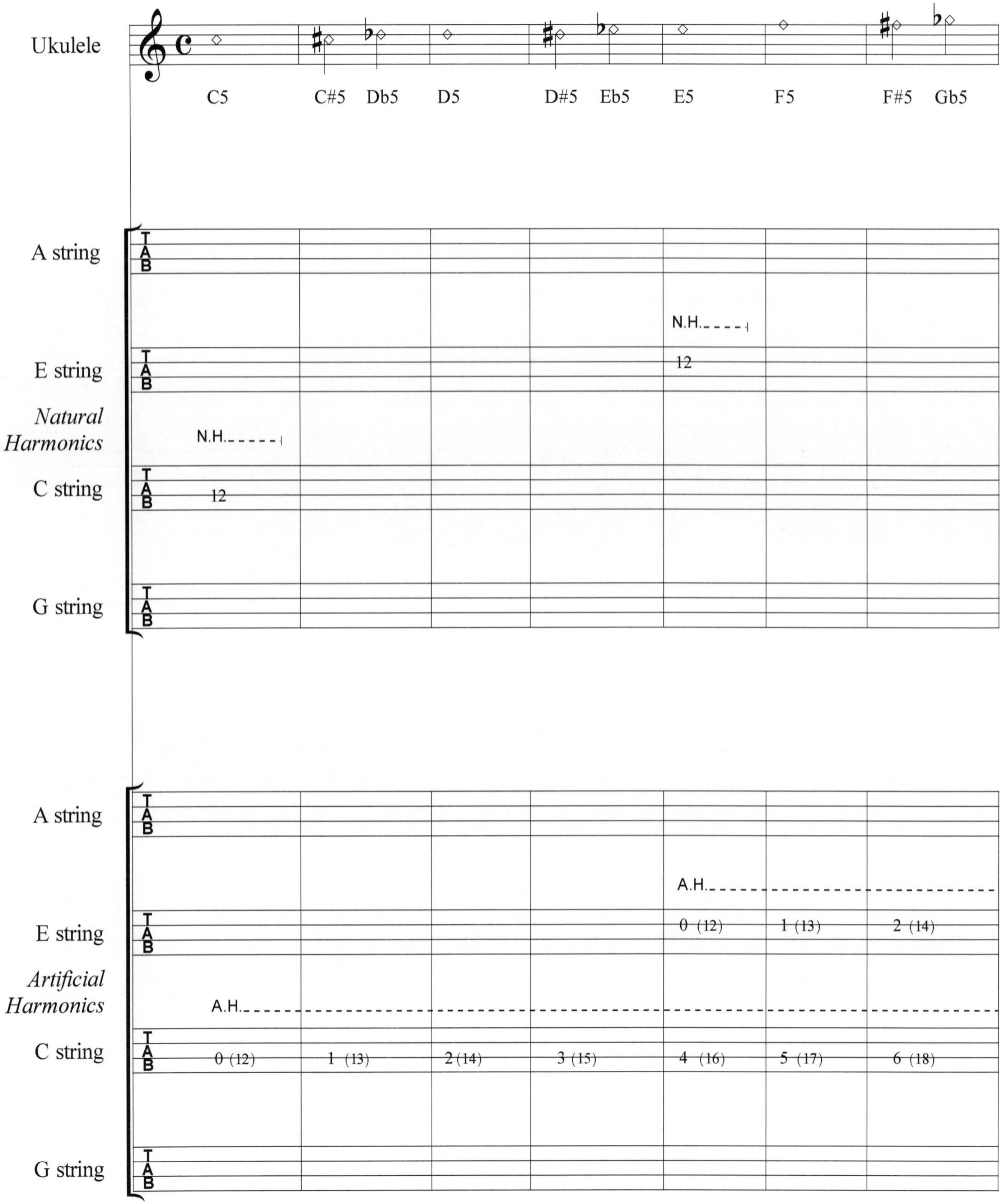

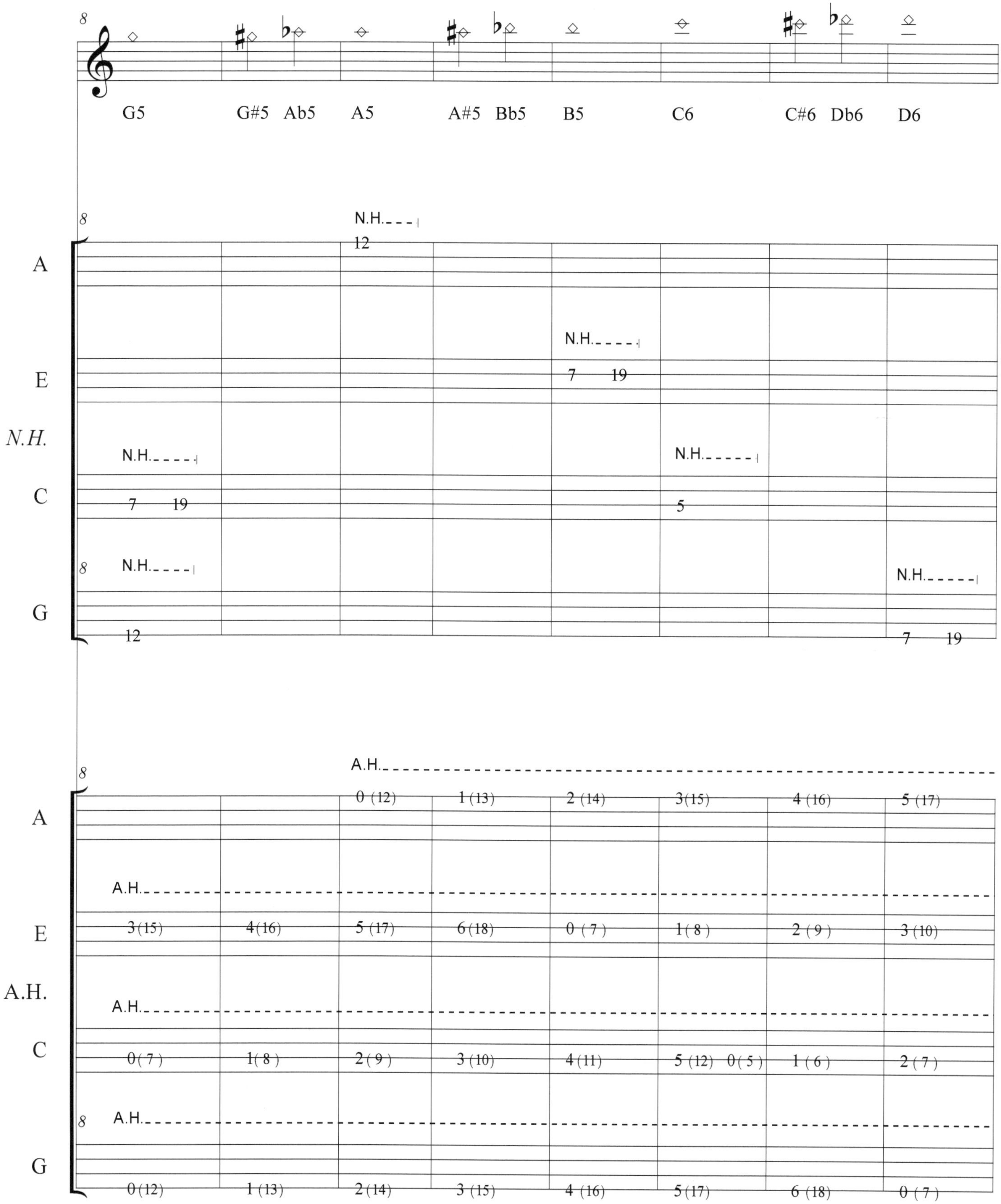
G5 G#5 Ab5 A5 A#5 Bb5 B5 C6 C#6 Db6 D6
A
E
N.H.
C
G
N.H.
12
7 19
5
A
E
A.H.
C
G
A.H.
0 (12) 1 (13) 2 (14) 3(15) 4 (16) 5 (17)
3(15) 4(16) 5 (17) 6(18) 0 (7) 1(8) 2 (9) 3 (10)
0(7) 1(8) 2 (9) 3 (10) 4 (11) 5 (12) 0(5) 1 (6) 2 (7)
0 (12) 1 (13) 2 (14) 3 (15) 4 (16) 5(17) 6 (18) 0 (7)

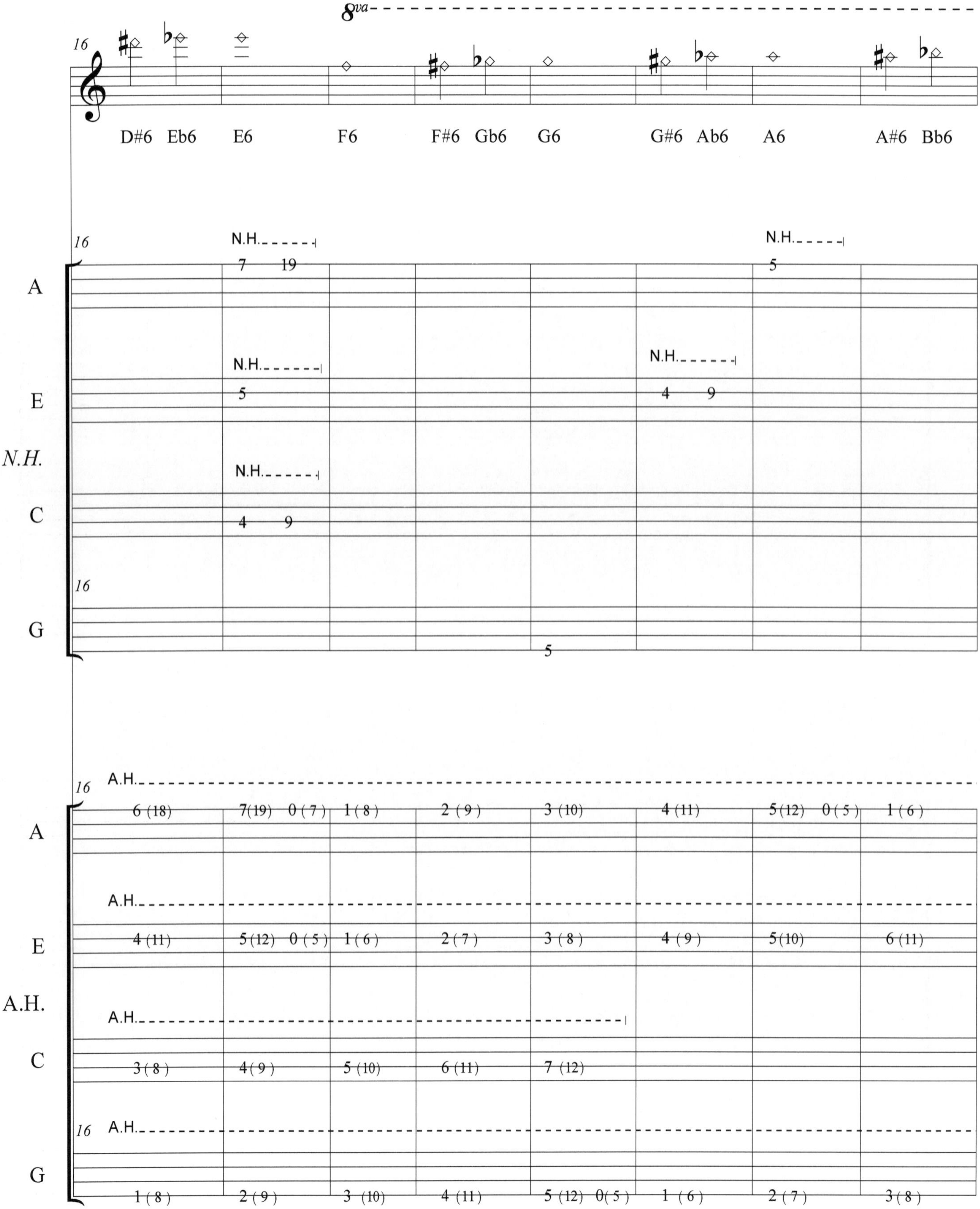
8va
16
D#6 Eb6 E6 F6 F#6 Gb6 G6 G#6 Ab6 A6 A#6 Bb6
N.H.
A
E
N.H.
C
G
7 19
5
4 9
5
4 9
5
A.H.
A
E
A.H.
C
G
6 (18) 7(19) 0 (7) 1 (8) 2 (9) 3 (10) 4 (11) 5(12) 0 (5) 1 (6)
4 (11) 5(12) 0 (5) 1 (6) 2 (7) 3 (8) 4 (9) 5(10) 6 (11)
3 (8) 4 (9) 5 (10) 6 (11) 7 (12)
1 (8) 2 (9) 3 (10) 4 (11) 5 (12) 0 (5) 1 (6) 2 (7) 3 (8)

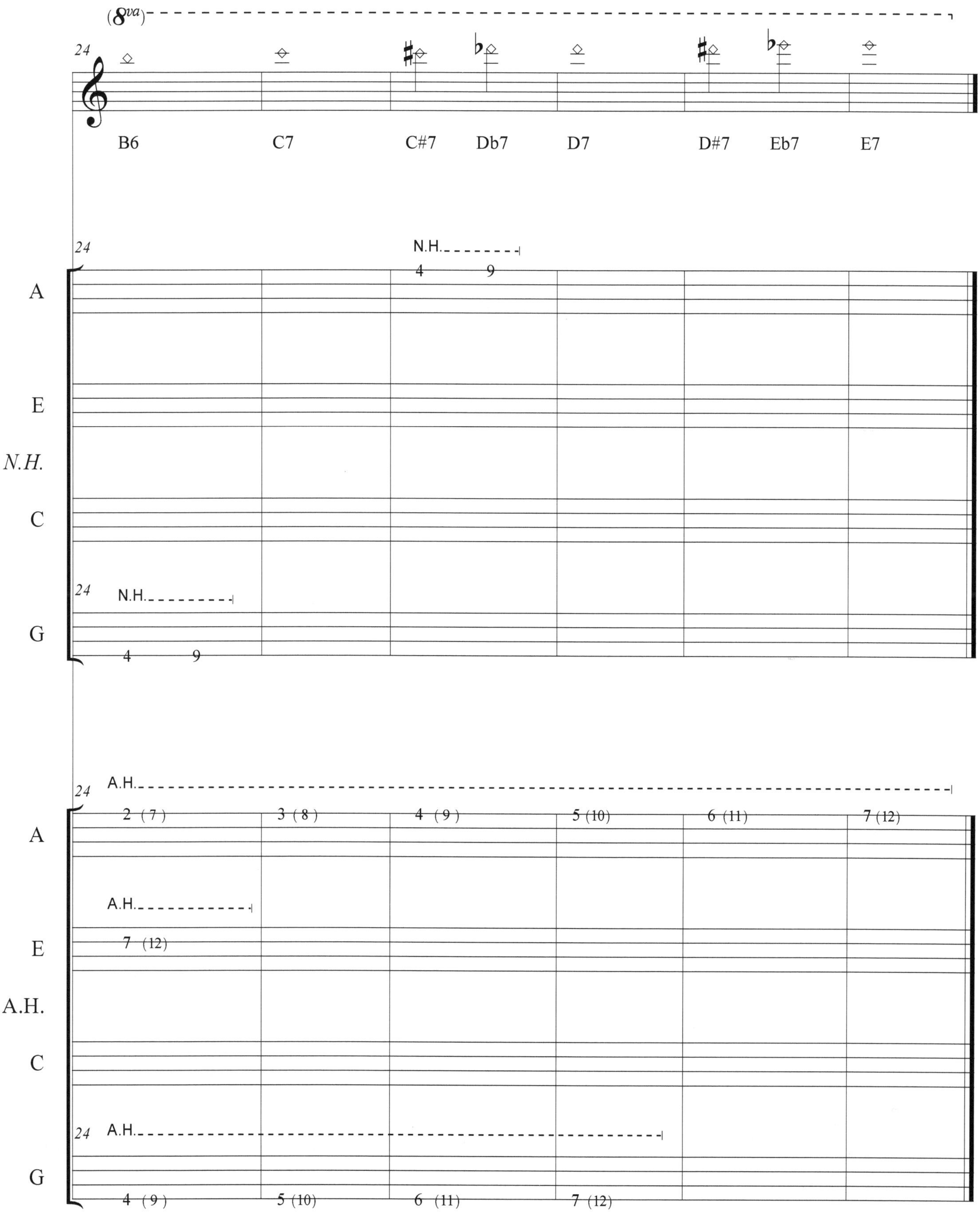
(8va)
24
B6
C7
C#7
Db7
D7
D#7
Eb7
E7
24
N.H.
4 9
A
E
N.H.
C
24
N.H.
G
4 9
24
A.H.
2 (7)
3 (8)
4 (9)
5 (10)
6 (11)
7 (12)
A
A.H.
E
7 (12)
A.H.
C
24
A.H.
G
4 (9)
5 (10)
6 (11)
7 (12)

Chords with only Natural Harmonics

Score

Ondřej Šárek

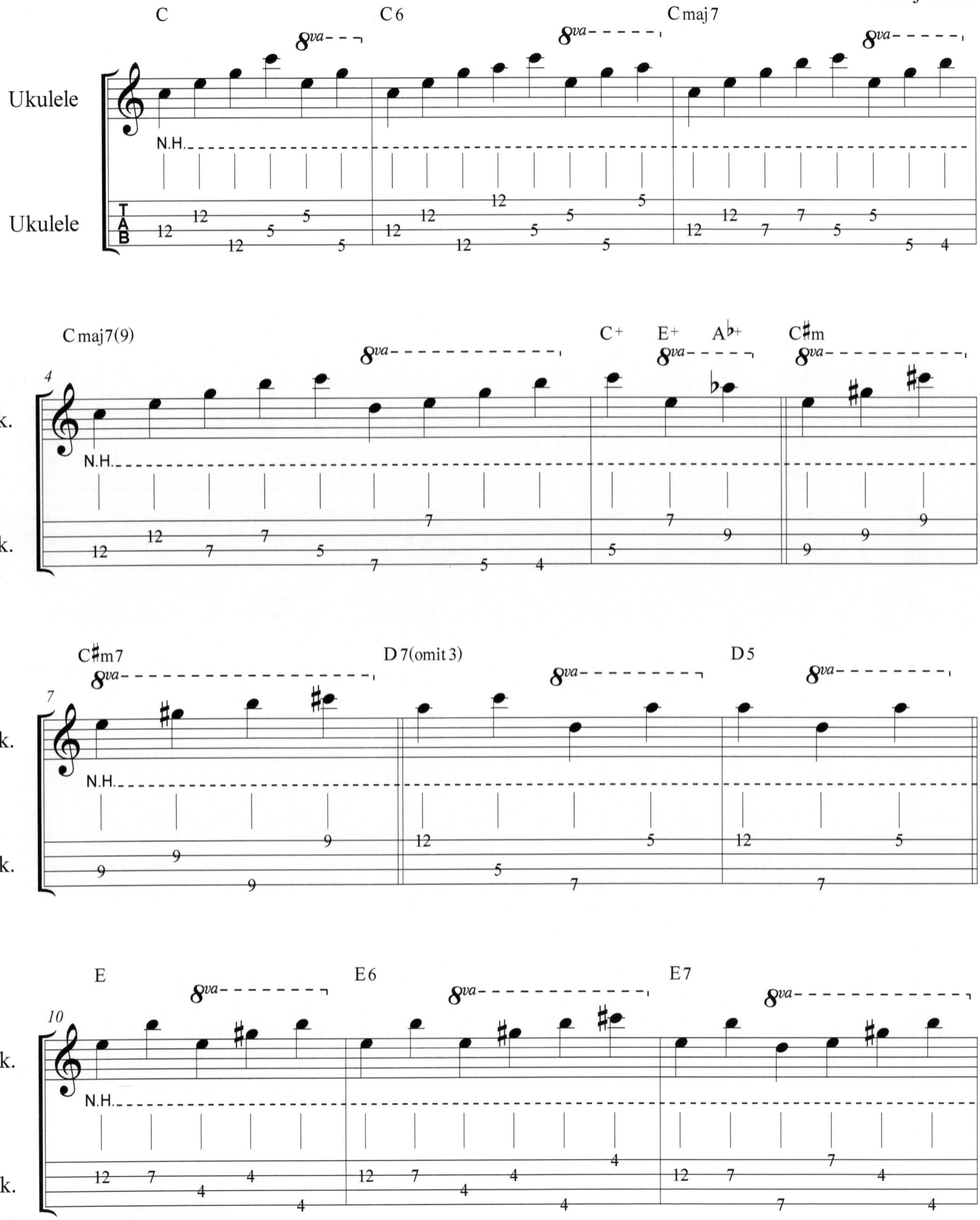

Chords with only Natural Harmonics

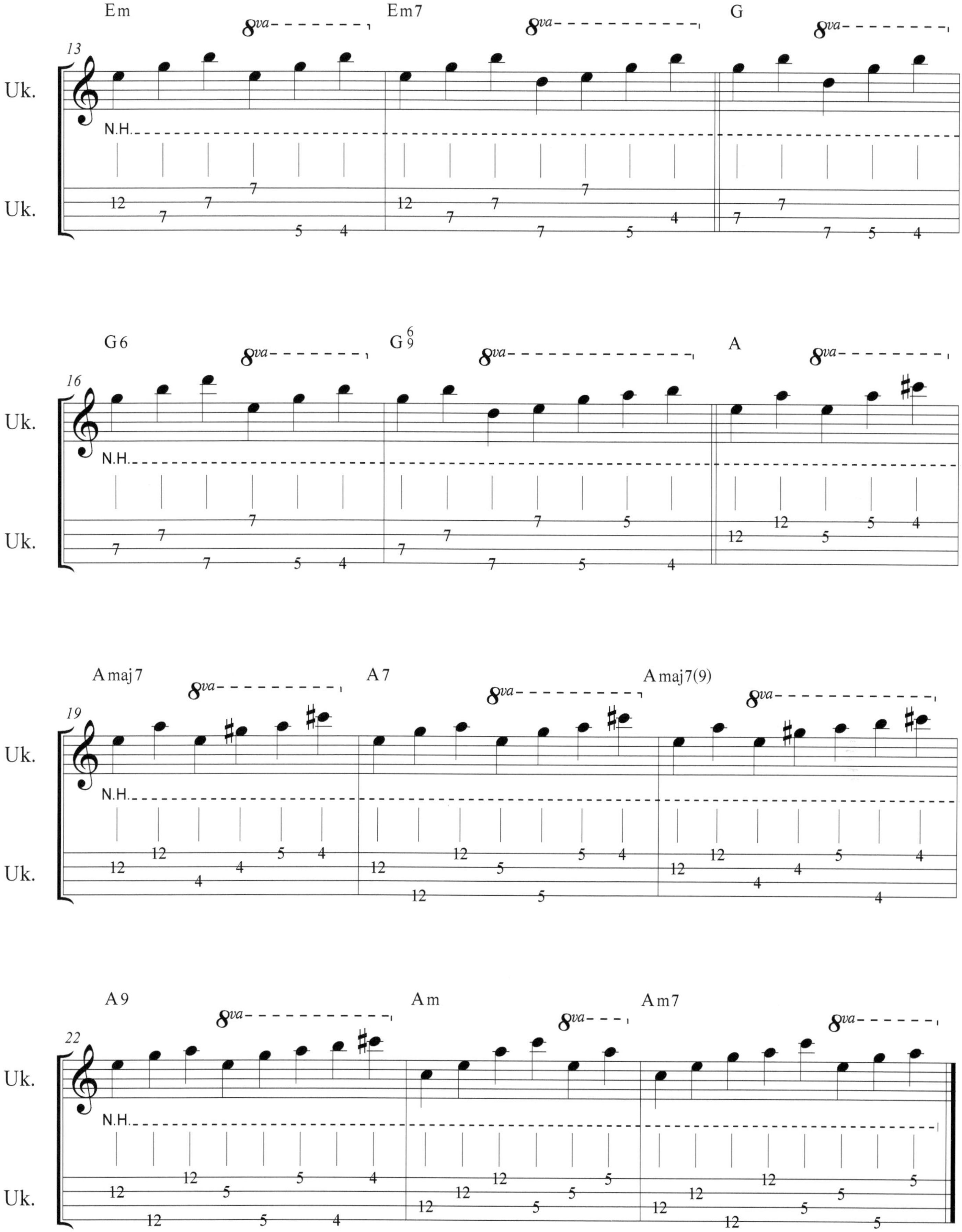

Major Arpeggios with Artificial Harmonics

Score

Ondřej Šárek

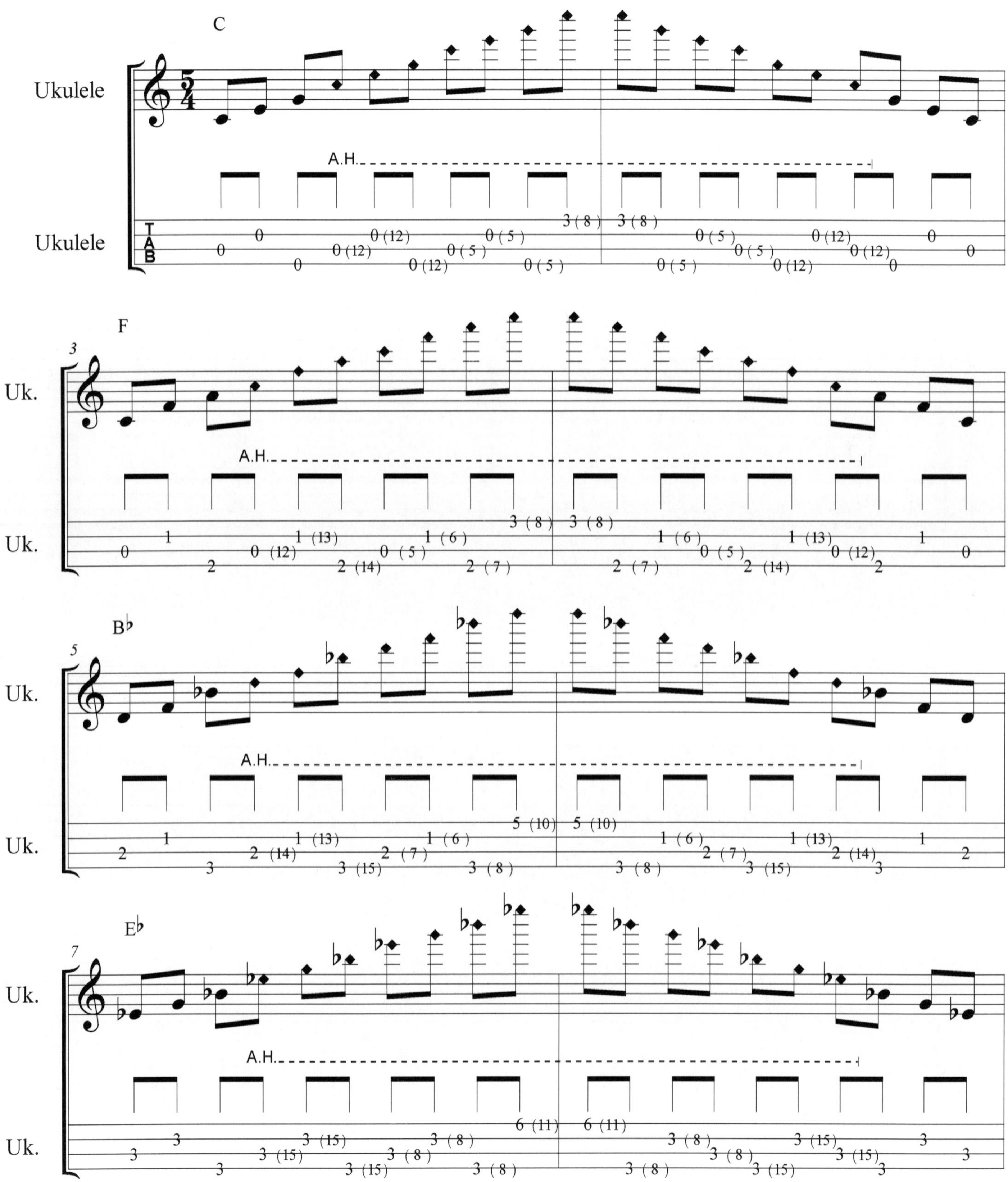

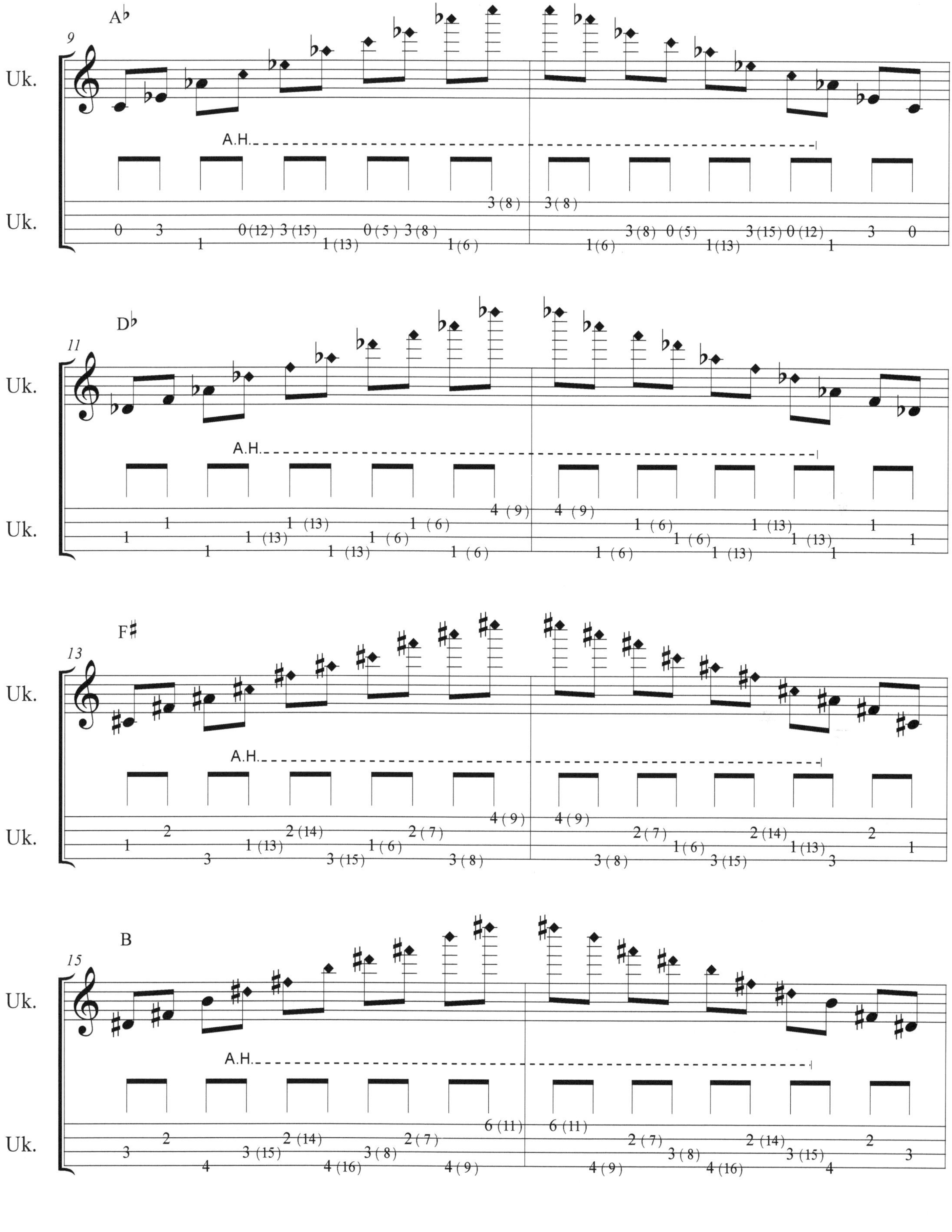
A♭
9
Uk.
A.H.
Uk.
D♭
11
Uk.
A.H.
Uk.
F♯
13
Uk.
A.H.
Uk.
B
15
Uk.
A.H.
Uk.

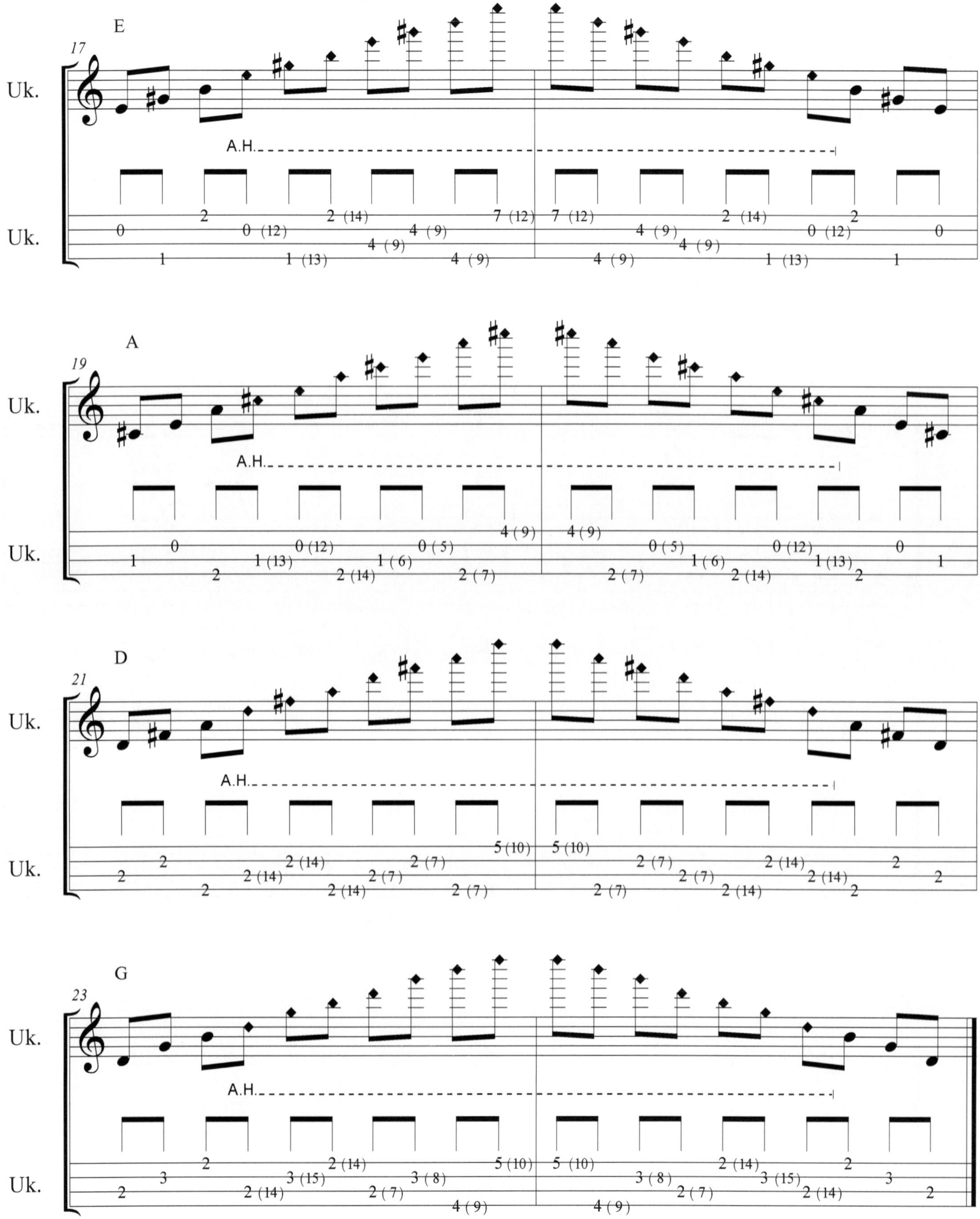
17
E
Uk.
A.H.
Uk.
19
A
Uk.
A.H.
Uk.
21
D
Uk.
A.H.
Uk.
23
G
Uk.
A.H.
Uk.

Score

Minor Arpeggios with Artificial Harmonics

Ondřej Šárek

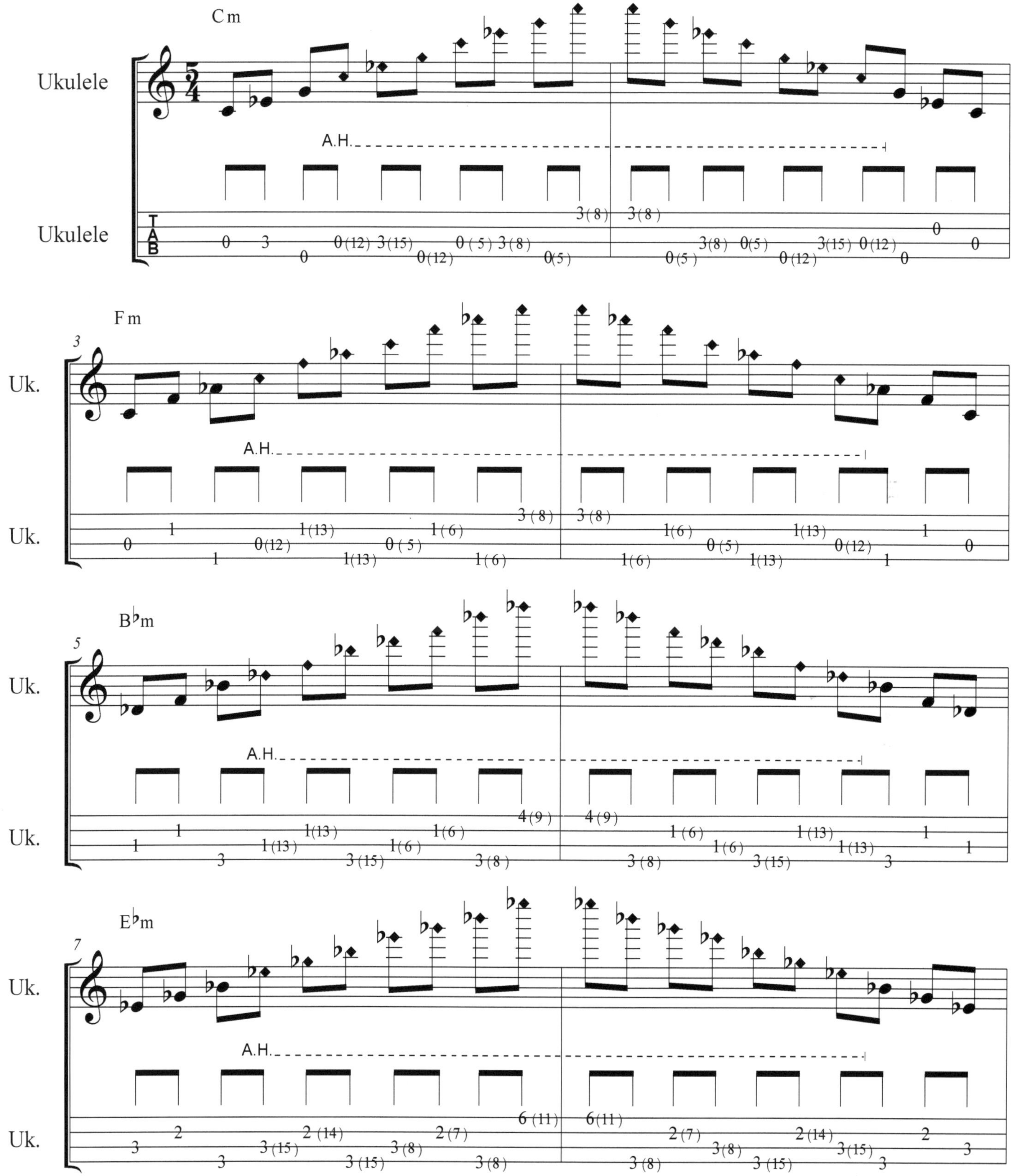

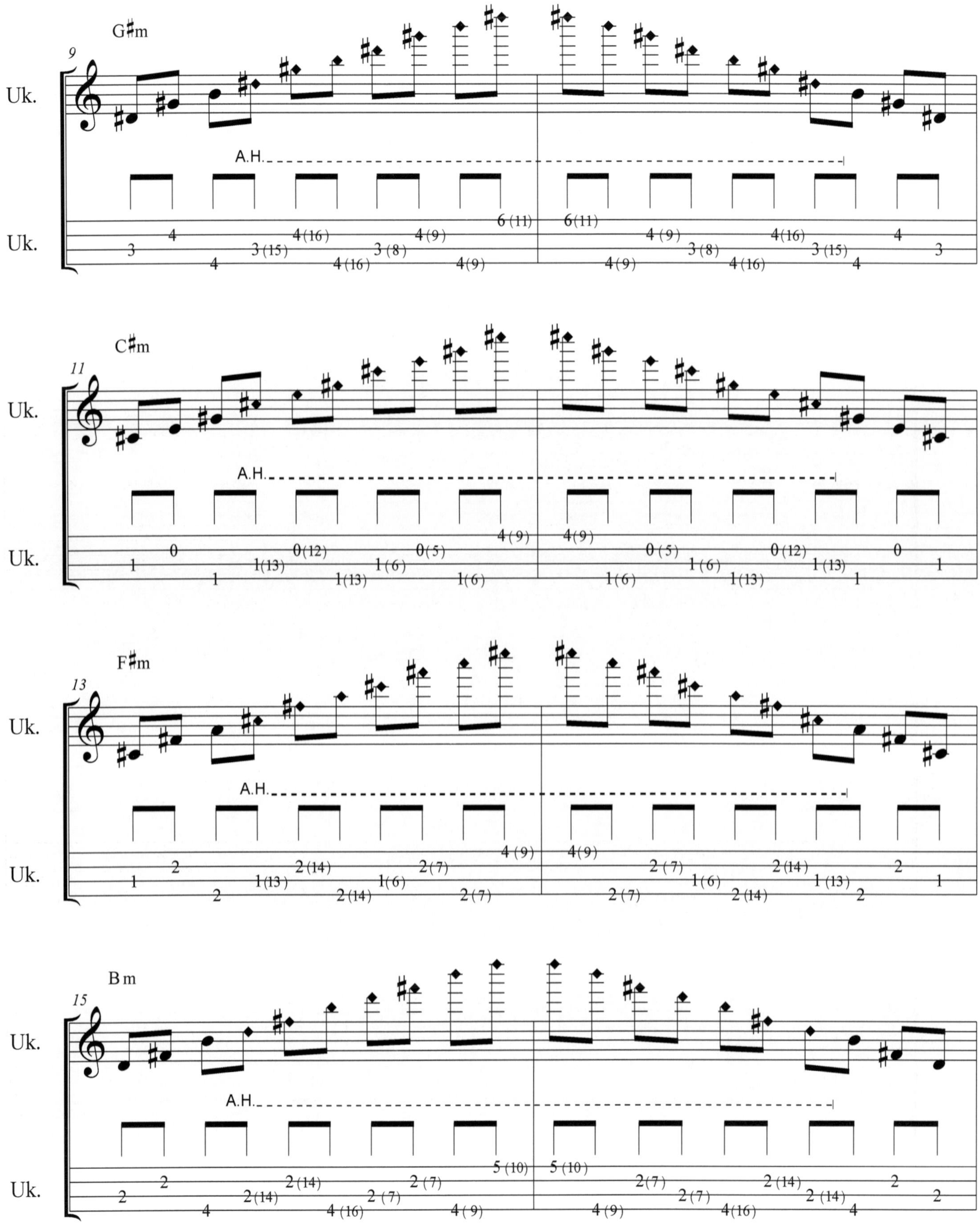
G♯m
9
Uk.
A.H.
Uk.
C♯m
11
Uk.
A.H.
Uk.
F♯m
13
Uk.
A.H.
Uk.
B m
15
Uk.
A.H.
Uk.

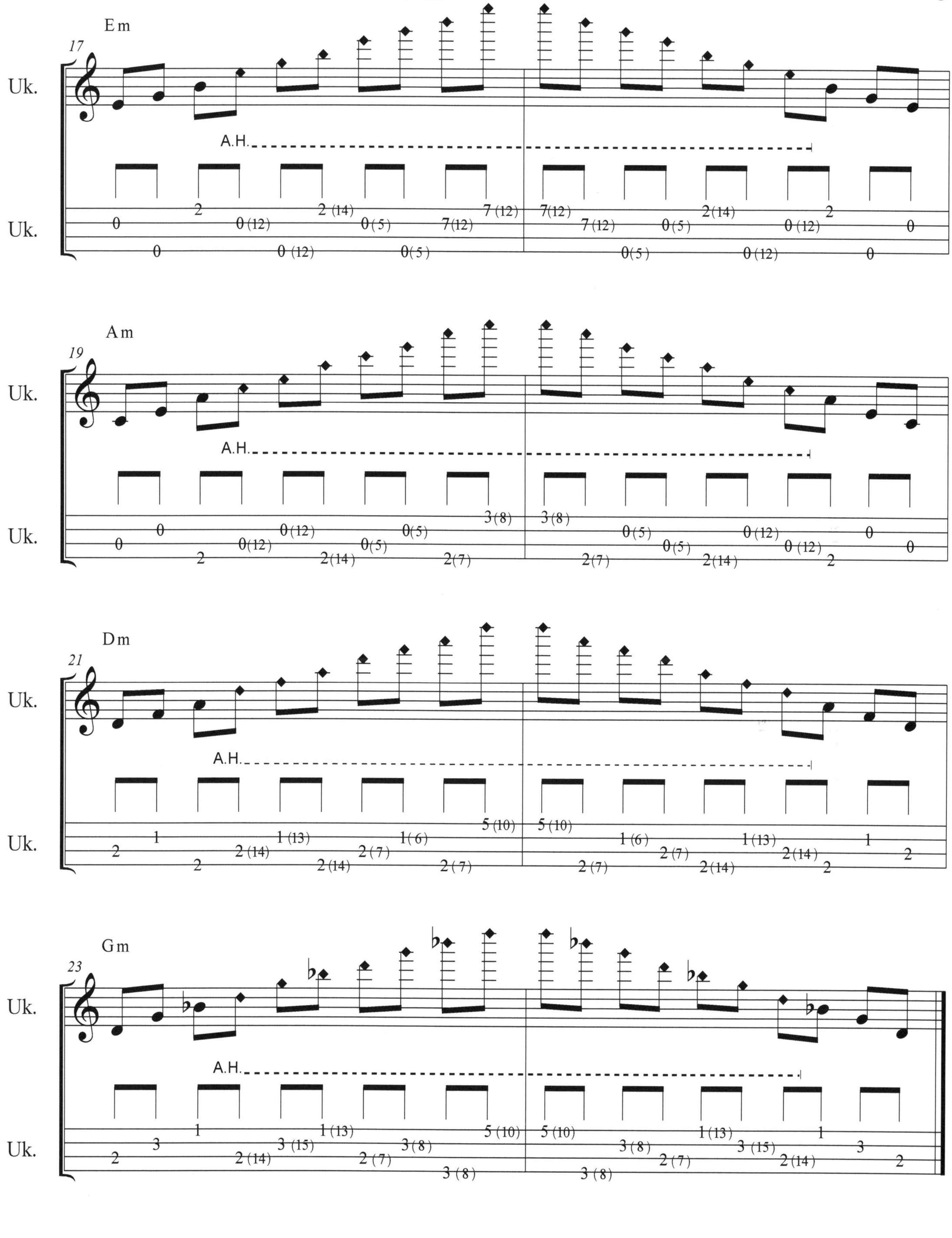
Em
17
Uk.
A.H.
Uk.
Am
19
Uk.
A.H.
Uk.
Dm
21
Uk.
A.H.
Uk.
Gm
23
Uk.
A.H.
Uk.

Another section is devoted to the accompaniments with harmonics. On four pages you will find sample of picking patterns with artificial harmonics. But it is true here that the patterns are for inspiration only , create your own rhythmic variations.

As inspiration , how to use patterns , I arragnged two songs (London Bridge , Lazy Mary) . For each melody there are two different accompaniments. There is also one example of the harmonics that can be used as a „fill -in" the basic accompaniment played by another instrument

Picking patterns with Artificial Harmonics

Score

Ondřej Šárek

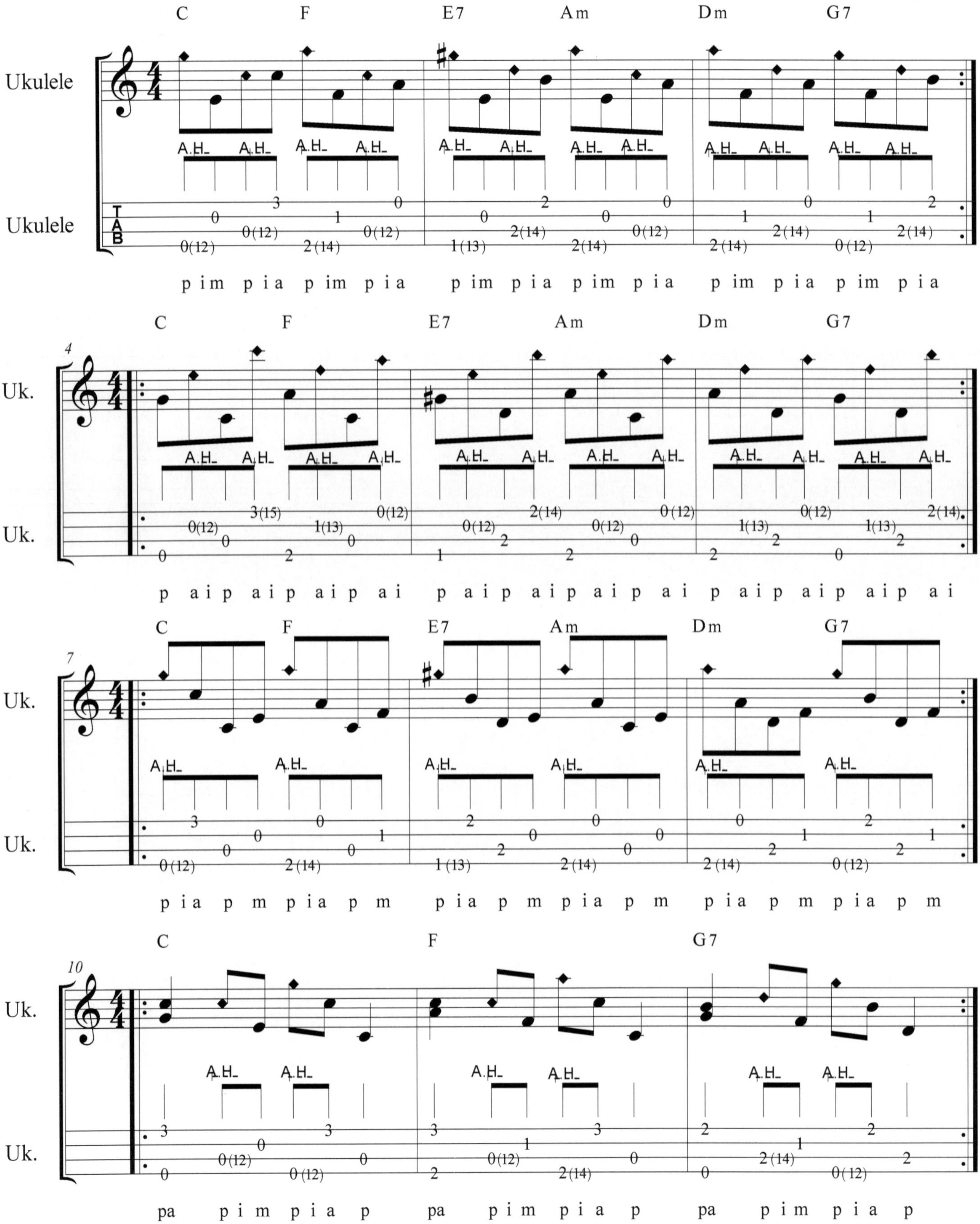

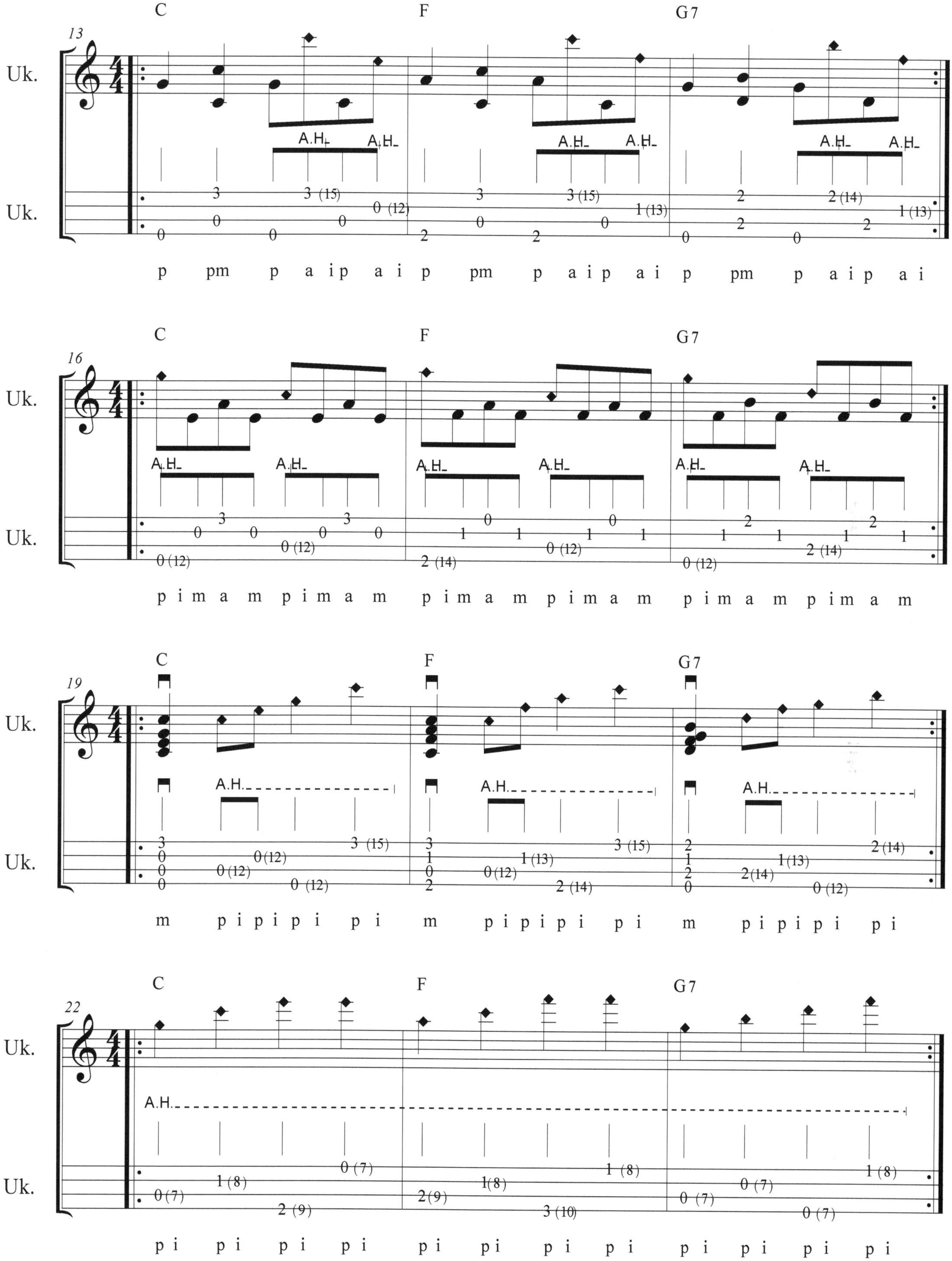
C F G7
13
Uk.
A.H. A.H. A.H. A.H. A.H. A.H.
Uk.
p pm p a i p a i p pm p a i p a i p pm p a i p a i
C F G7
16
Uk.
A.H. A.H. A.H. A.H. A.H. A.H.
Uk.
p i m a m p i m a m p i m a m p i m a m p i m a m p i m a m
C F G7
19
Uk.
A.H. A.H. A.H.
Uk.
m p i p i p i p i m p i p i p i p i m p i p i p i p i
C F G7
22
Uk.
A.H.
Uk.
p i p i p i p i p i p i p i p i p i p i p i p i

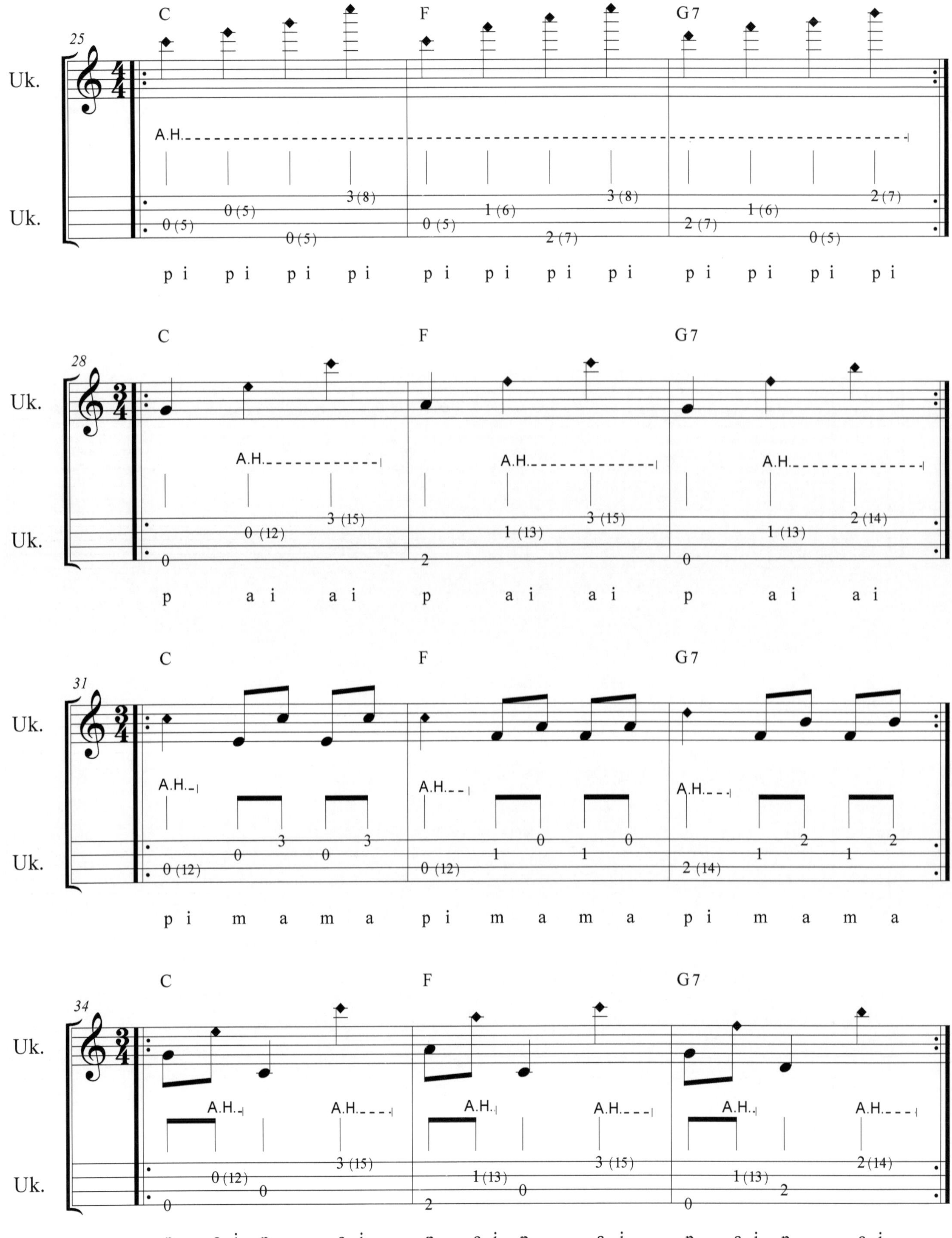
C F G7
Uk.
Uk.
A.H.
p i p i p i p i p i p i p i p i p i p i p i p i
C F G7
p a i a i p a i a i p a i a i
C F G7
p i m a m a p i m a m a p i m a m a
C F G7

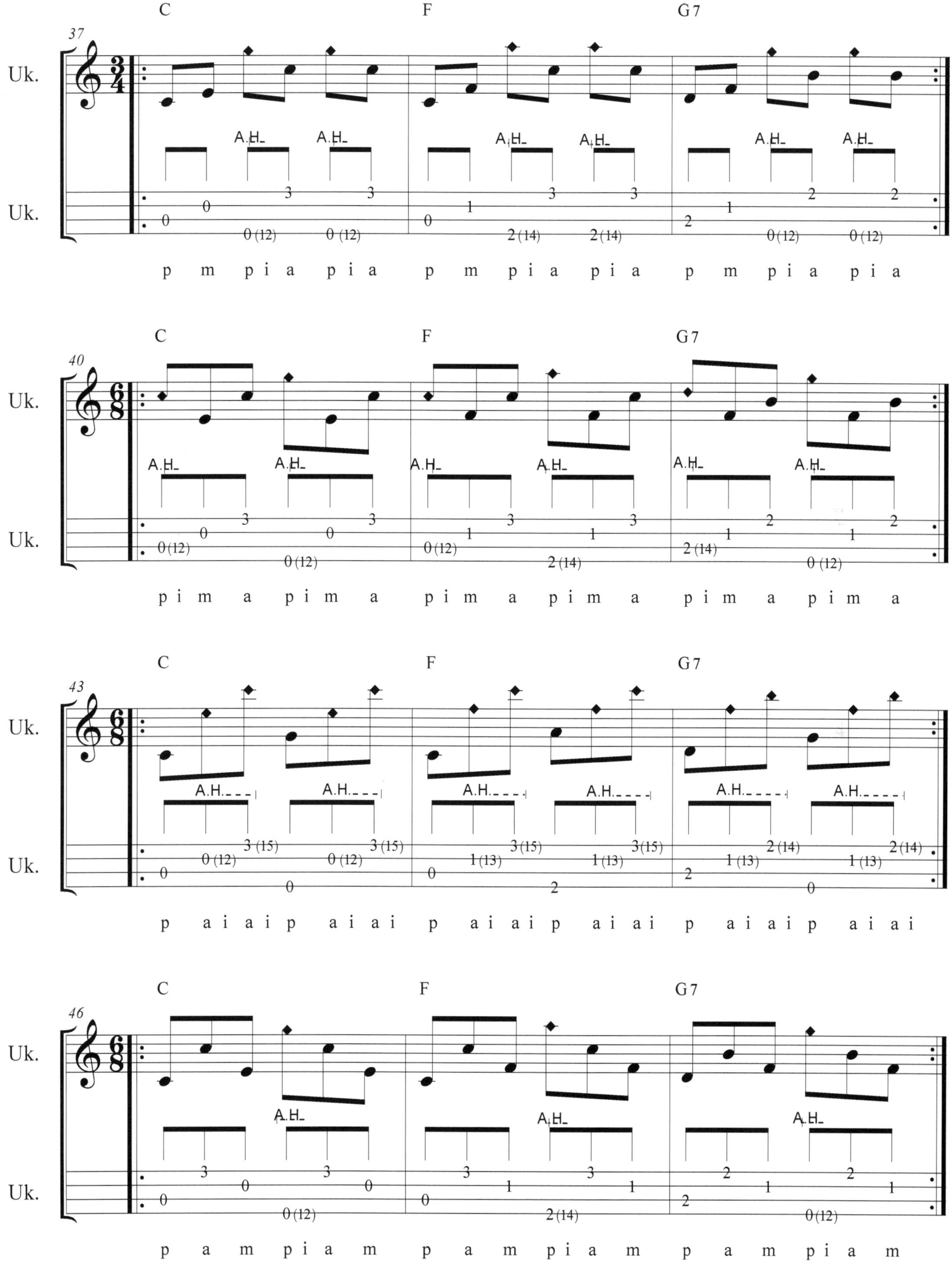
C
F
G7
37
Uk.
Uk.
A.H.
p m p i a p i a p m p i a p i a p m p i a p i a
40
p i m a p i m a p i m a p i m a p i m a p i m a
43
p a i a i p a i a i p a i a i p a i a i p a i a i p a i a i
46
p a m p i a m p a m p i a m p a m p i a m

London Bridge

English folk song
arr: Ondřej Šárek

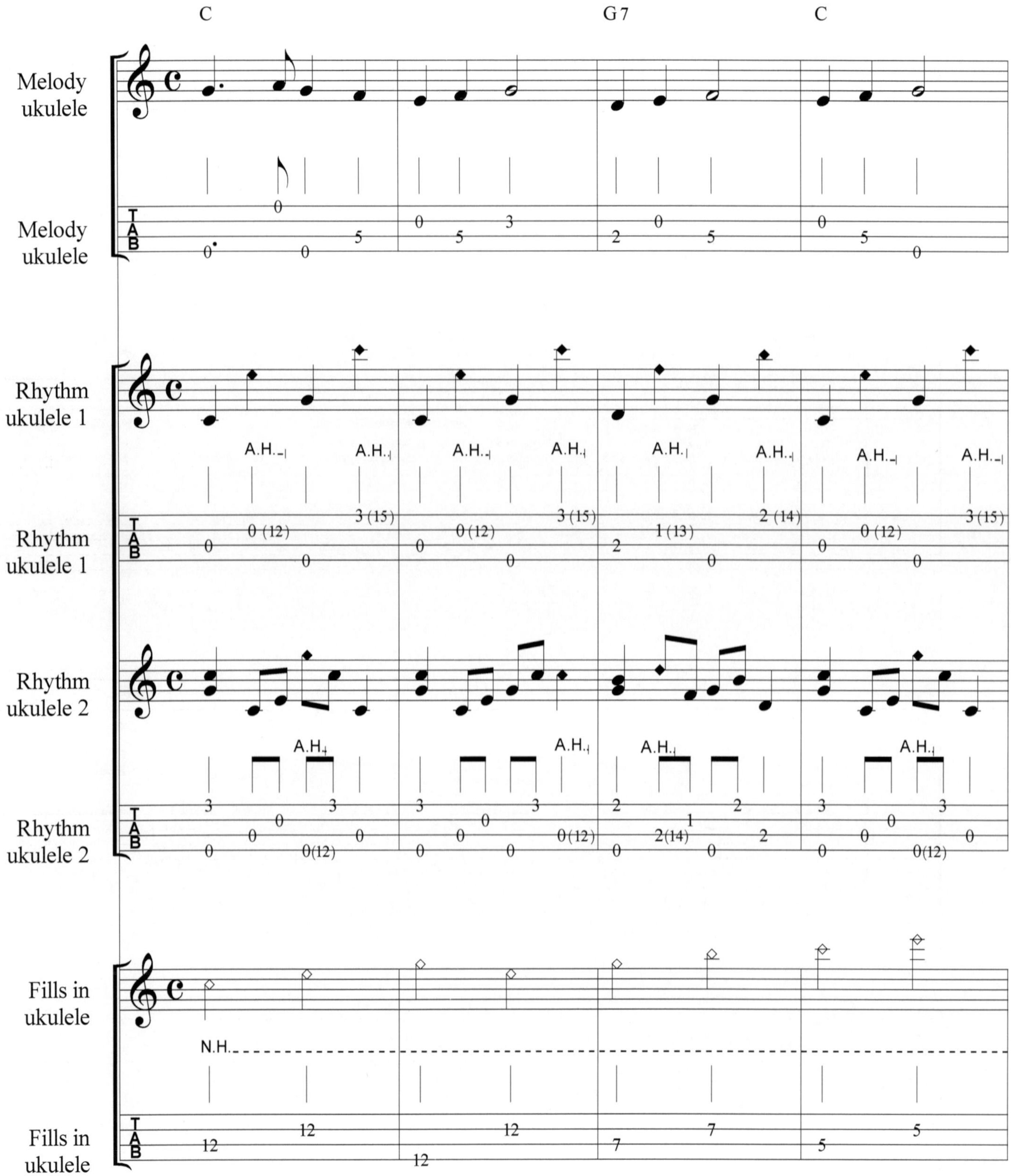

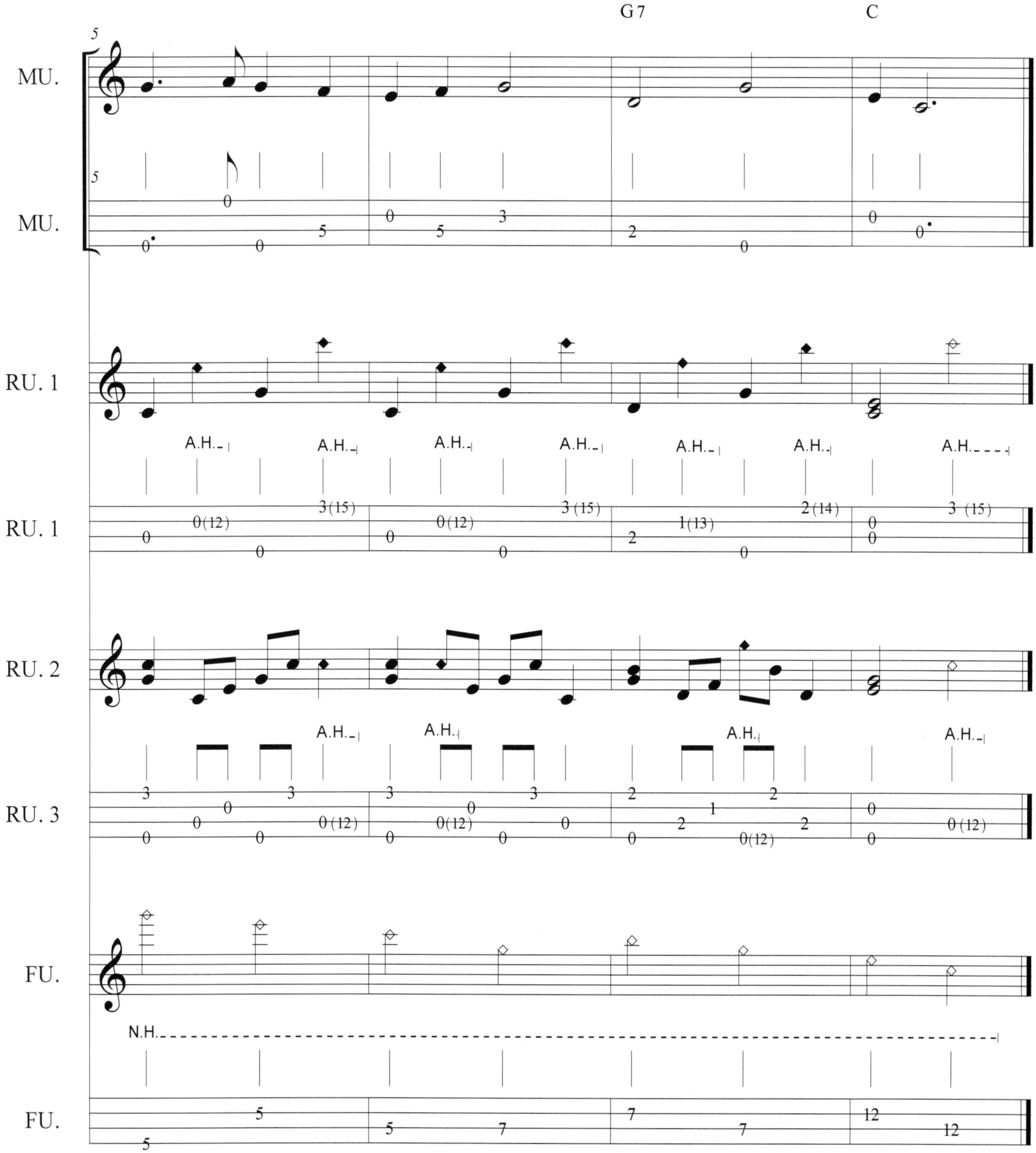
G 7
C
MU.
MU.
RU. 1
A.H.
RU. 1
RU. 2
A.H.
RU. 3
FU.
N.H.
FU.

Lazy Mary

English nursery song
arr: Ondřej Šárek

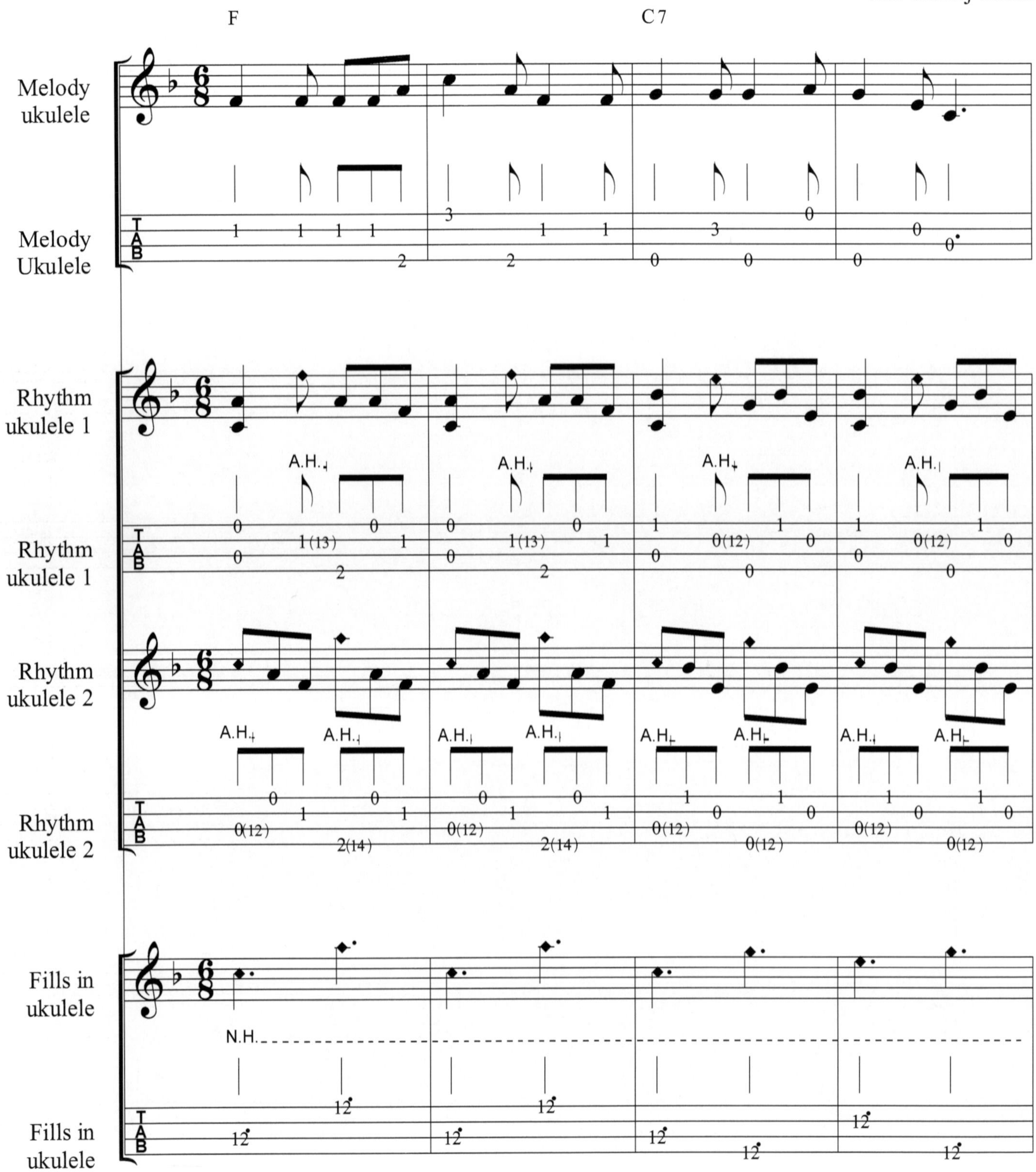

F
C 7
F
MU.
MU.
RU. 1
A.H.
RU. 1
RU 2.
A.H.
RU 2.
FU.
N.H.
FU.

Songbook

The last part of the book provides a songbook with the use of harmonics. For those who are interested I point out to some interesting use of harmonics.

1) The most commonly encountered harmonics is in the case when the melody goes too high and at the moment there is a need to play a few notes through the harmonics (Kesh jig) .
2) Play the entire melody only by the natural harmonics either in monophonic(Kerry polka) or homophony (Michael, Row The Boat Ashore) .
3) Play the song using natural harmonics and missing tones to complement by the non - harmonics tones (Mary Had A Little Lamb) .
4) Play a song in a chord style and melody to play using harmonics (Nearer , My God , to Thee) .
5) Combine Carter style with harmonics (Tum Balalaika) .
6) Polyphony style , the melody in the upper voice uses harmonics. (Humoresques) .
7) Polyphony style , the melody is in a lower voice and uses harmonics. (The Streets of Laredo)
8) Use only harmonics to „fill -in „ (Santa Lucia) .

Of course, these options can be combined and I highly recommend it .

Amazing Grace

Christian hymn
arr: Ondřej Šárek

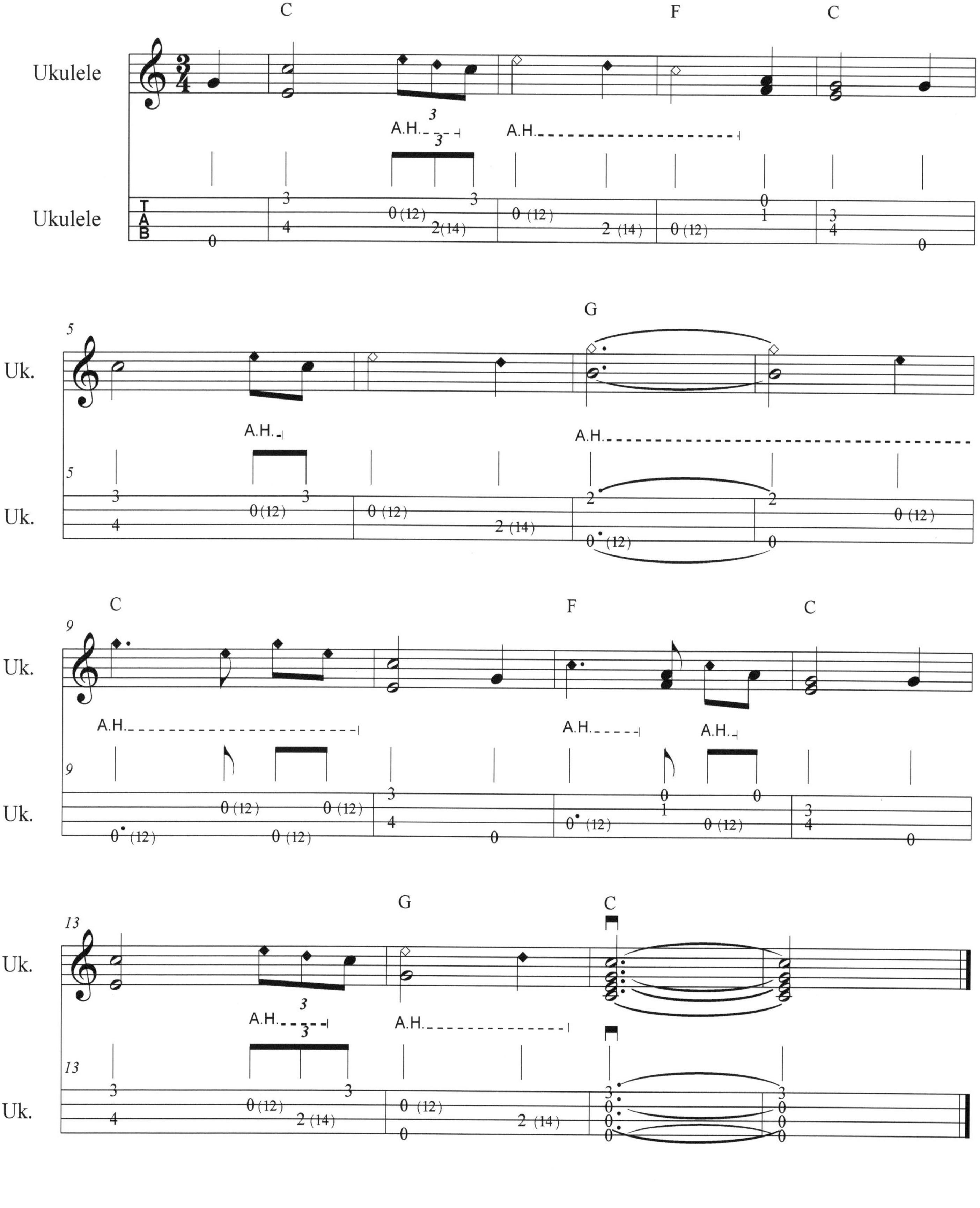

An der schönen blauen Donau

(Main Theme)

Score

Johann Strauss II
arr: Ondřej Šárek

17
Uk.
A.H.
A.H.
Uk.
G6
21
Uk.
A.H.
A.H.
Uk.
Em
A9
D
25
Uk.
A.H.
Uk.
G6
A9
D
29
Uk.
Uk.

Auld Lang Syne

Score

Robert Burns
arr: Ondřej Šárek

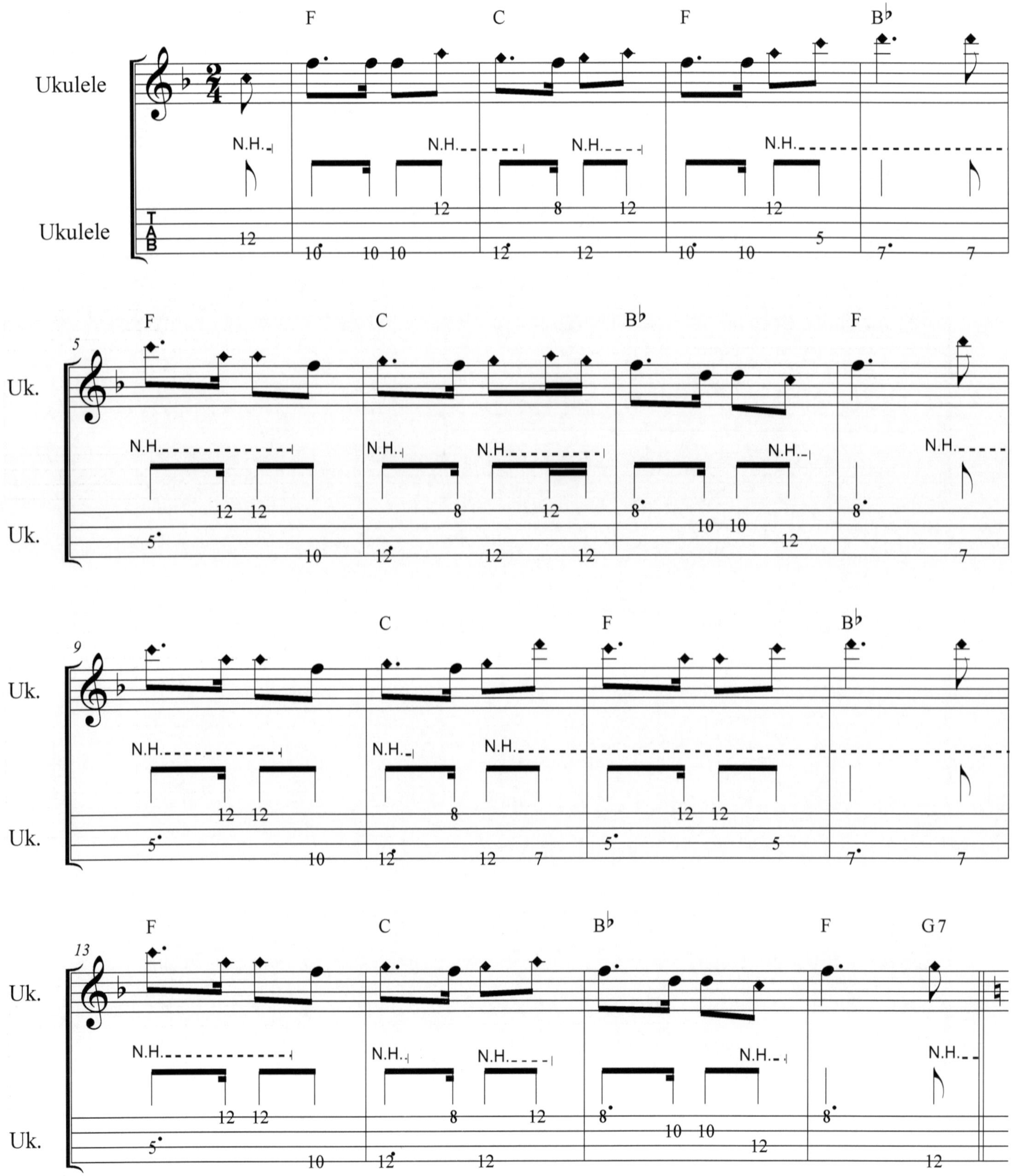

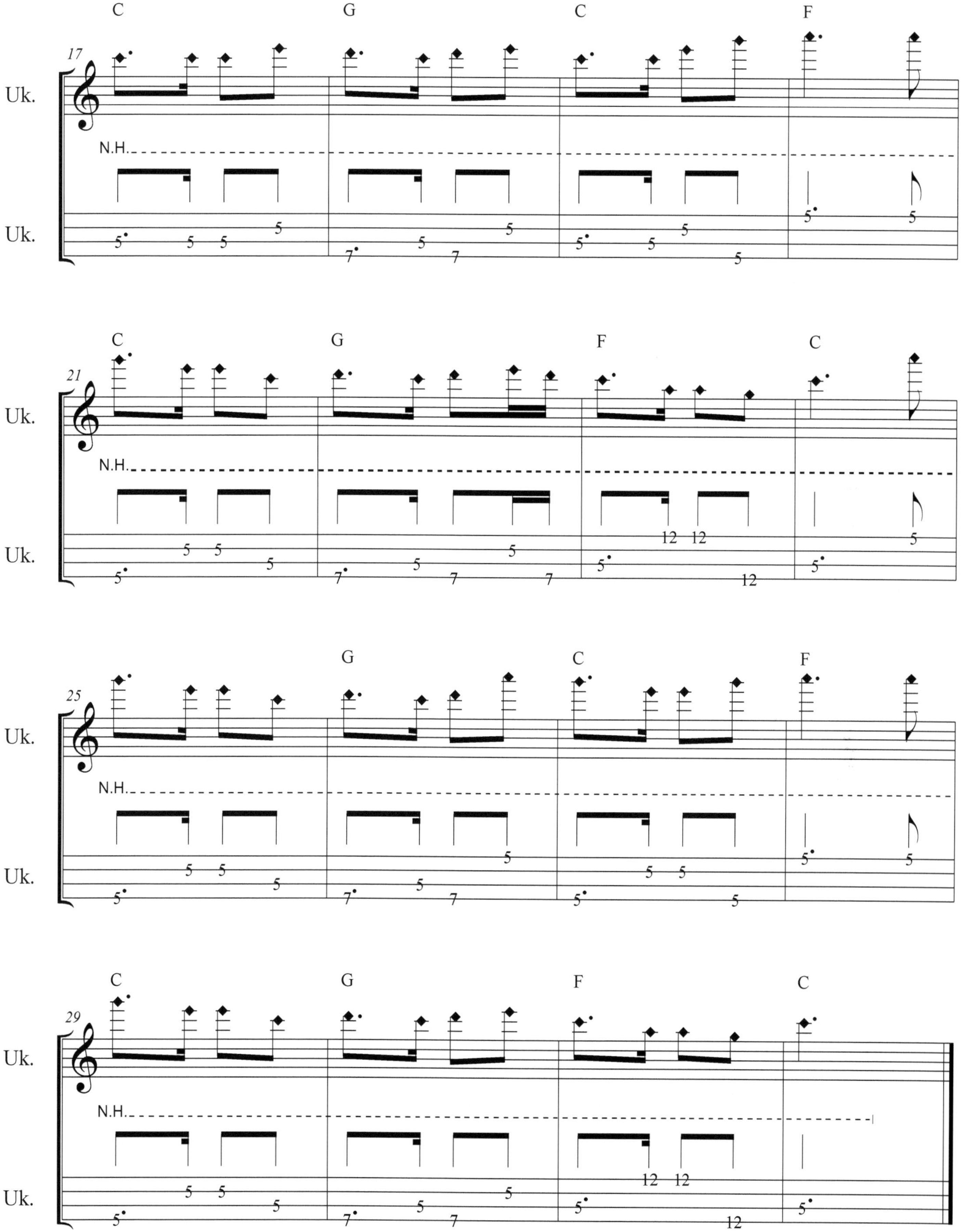
C G C F
17
Uk.
N.H.
Uk.
C G F C
21
Uk.
N.H.
Uk.
G C F
25
Uk.
N.H.
Uk.
C G F C
29
Uk.
N.H.
Uk.

Blackberry Blossom

American folk song
arr: Ondřej Šárek

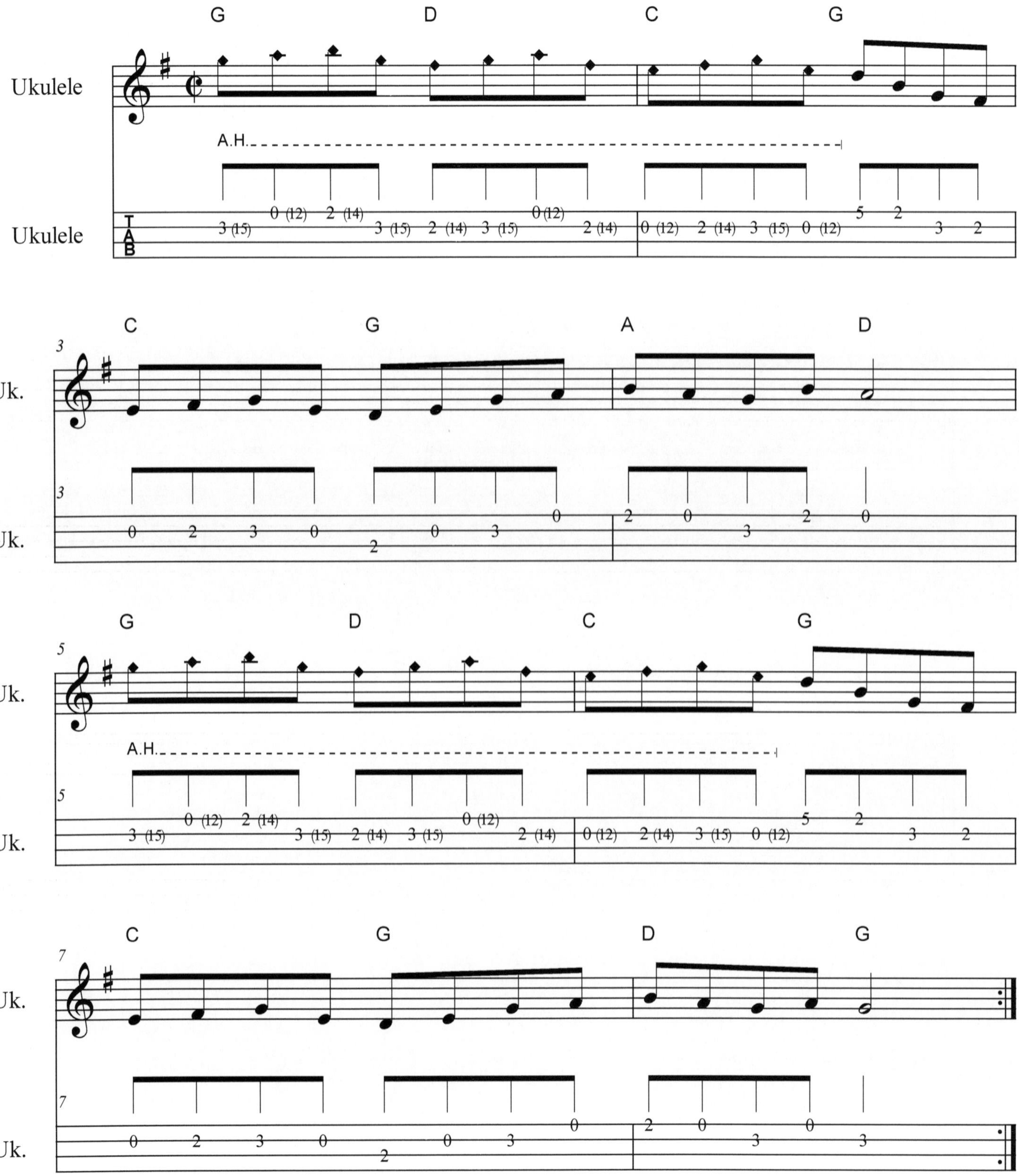

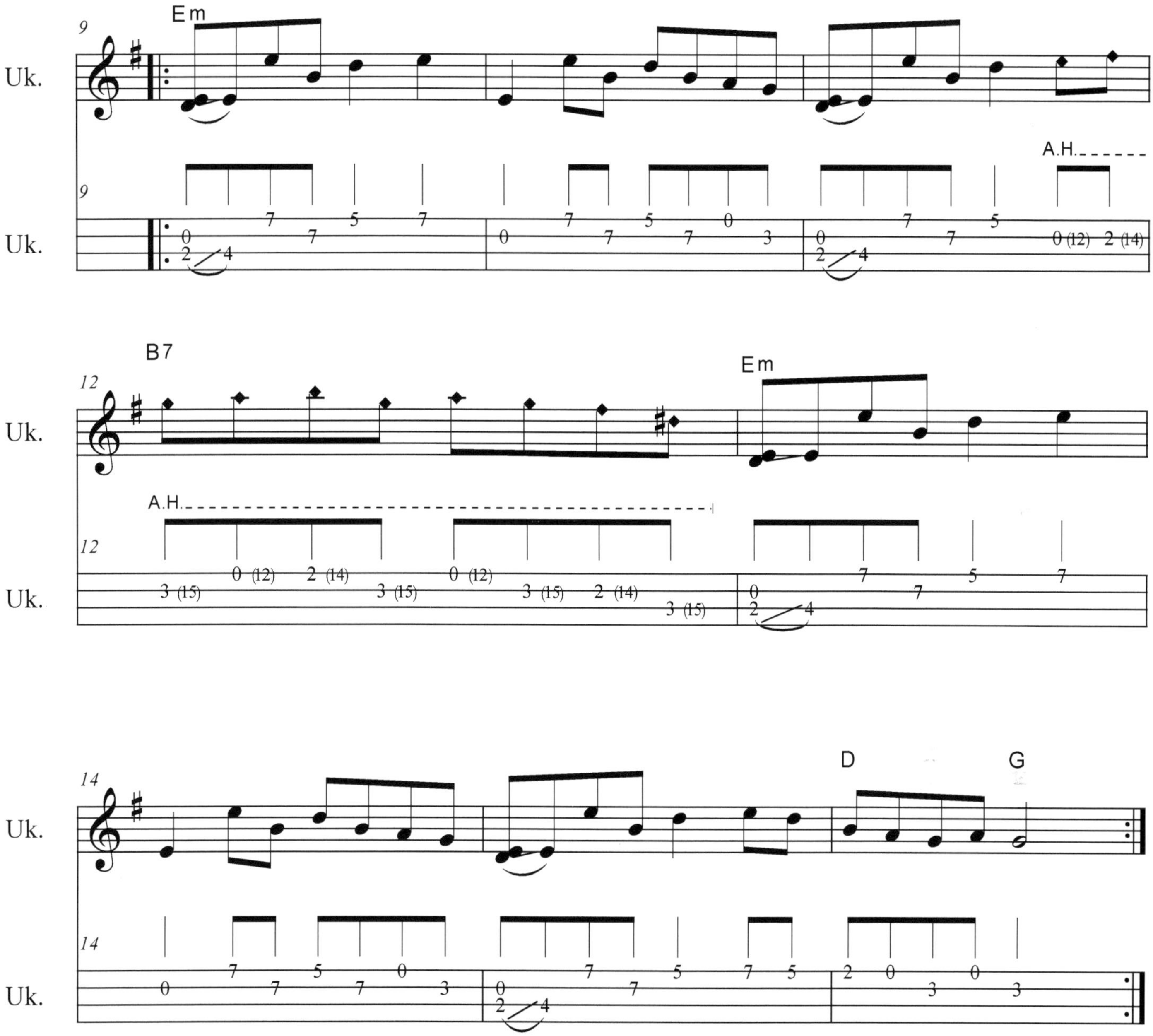
Em
Uk.
A.H.
B7
Em
D
G

Careless Love

Score

American blues song
arr: Ondřej Šárek

Drunten im Unterland

Score

German folk song
arr: Ondřej Šárek

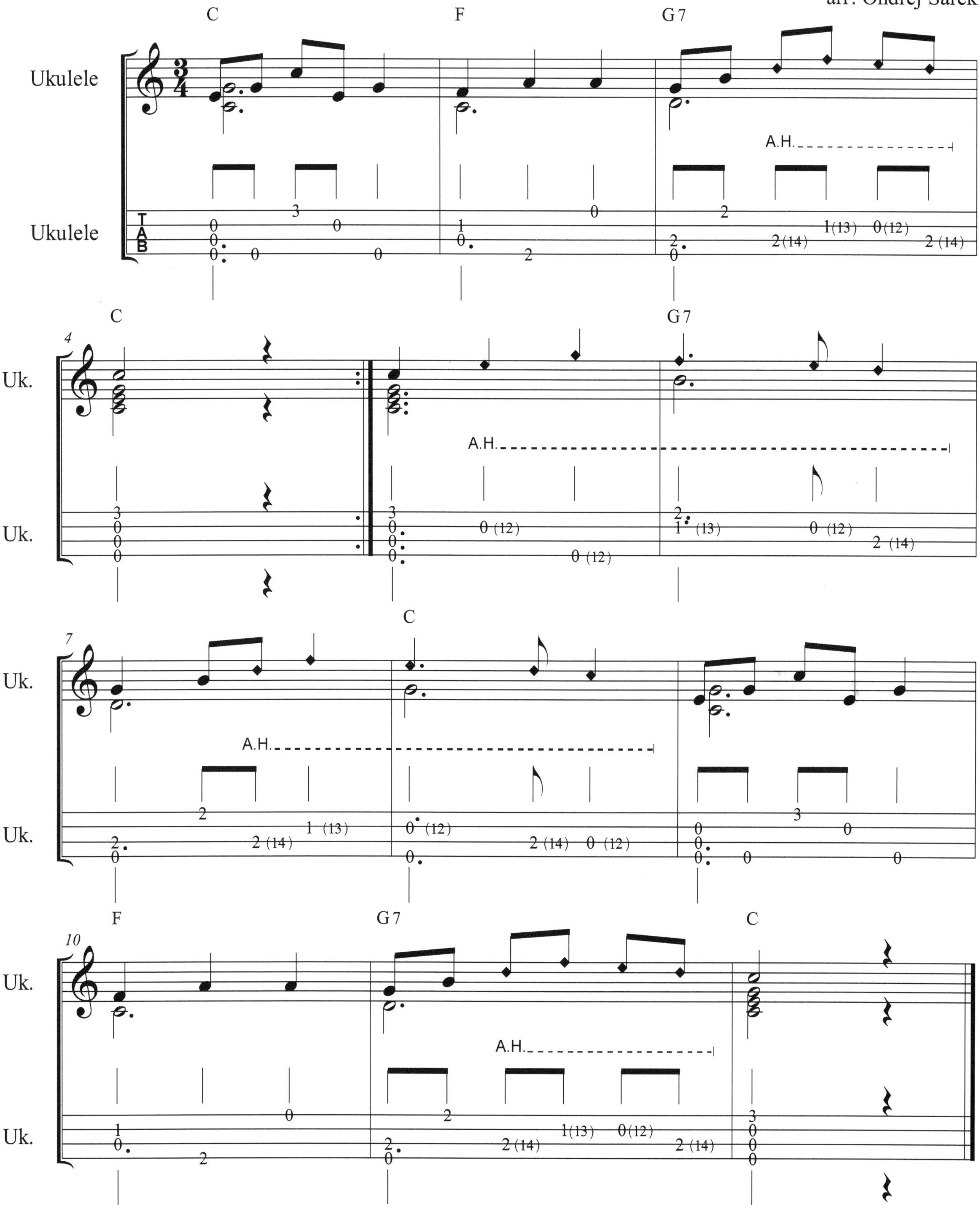

Score

Humoresques

op. 101, no. 7. (Main Theme)

Antonín Dvořák
arr: Ondřej Šárek

13
B7 Em C E7 Am D7
Uk.
A.H.
Uk.
16
B7 Em7(♭5) A7 D7 G C
Uk.
A.H.
Uk.
19
G D7 G
Uk.
A.H.
A.H.
Uk.
22
C G Gm Gdim D7 G
Uk.
A.H.
Uk.

Frankie and Johnny

Score

American blues song
arr: Ondřej Šárek

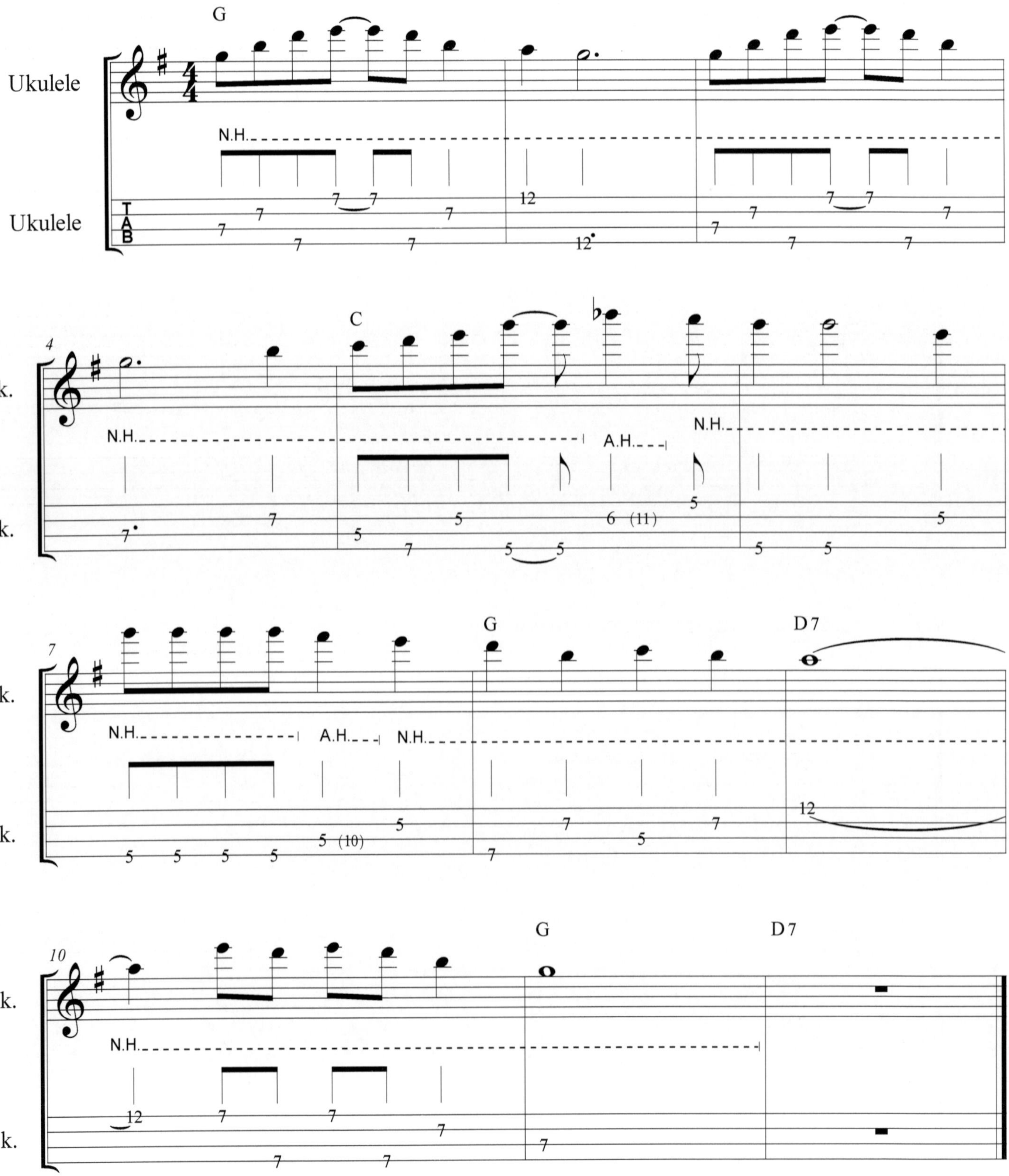

Johnny Micky's

Score

Irish polka
arr: Ondřej Šárek

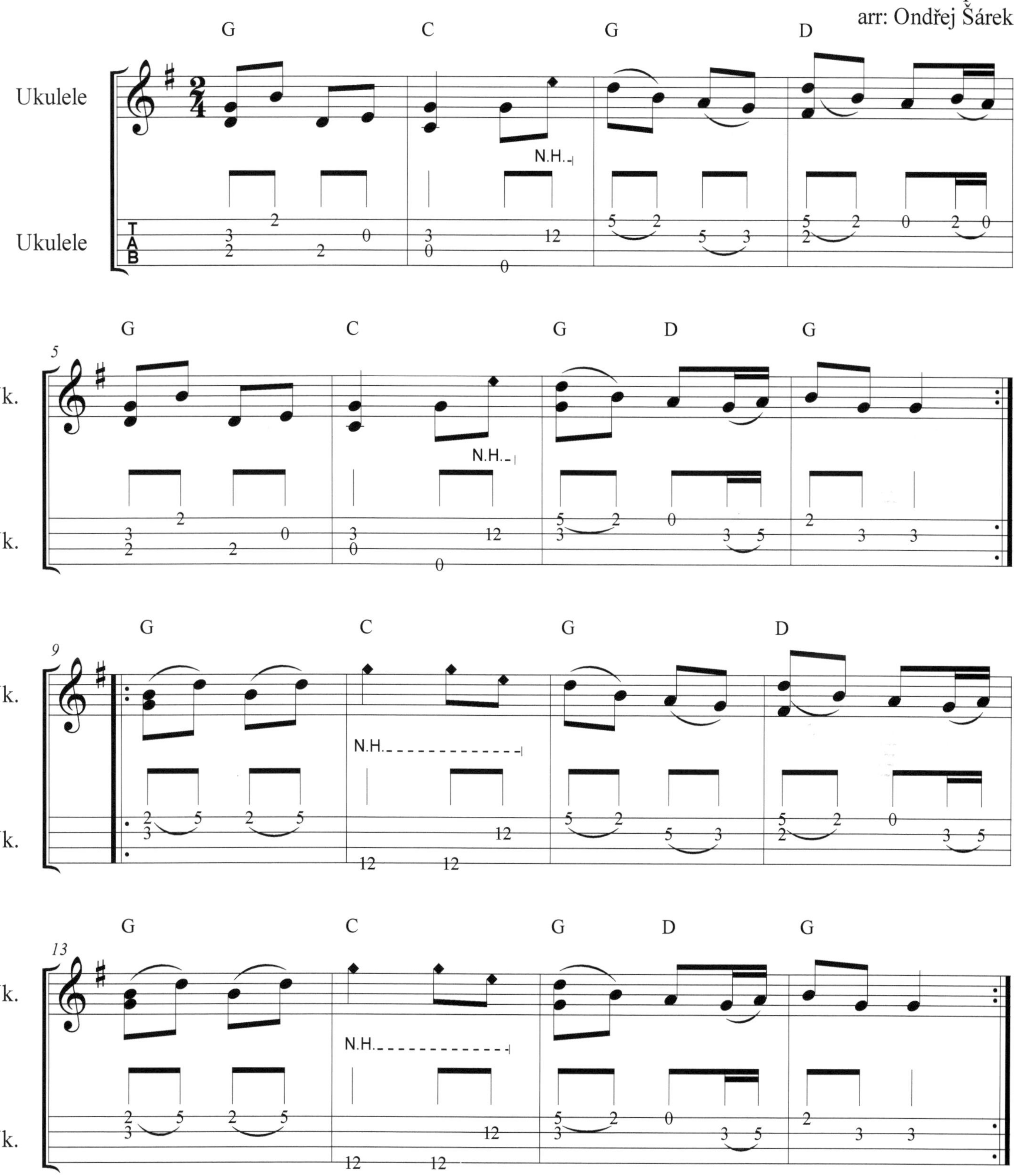

Kerry Polka

Score

Irish polka

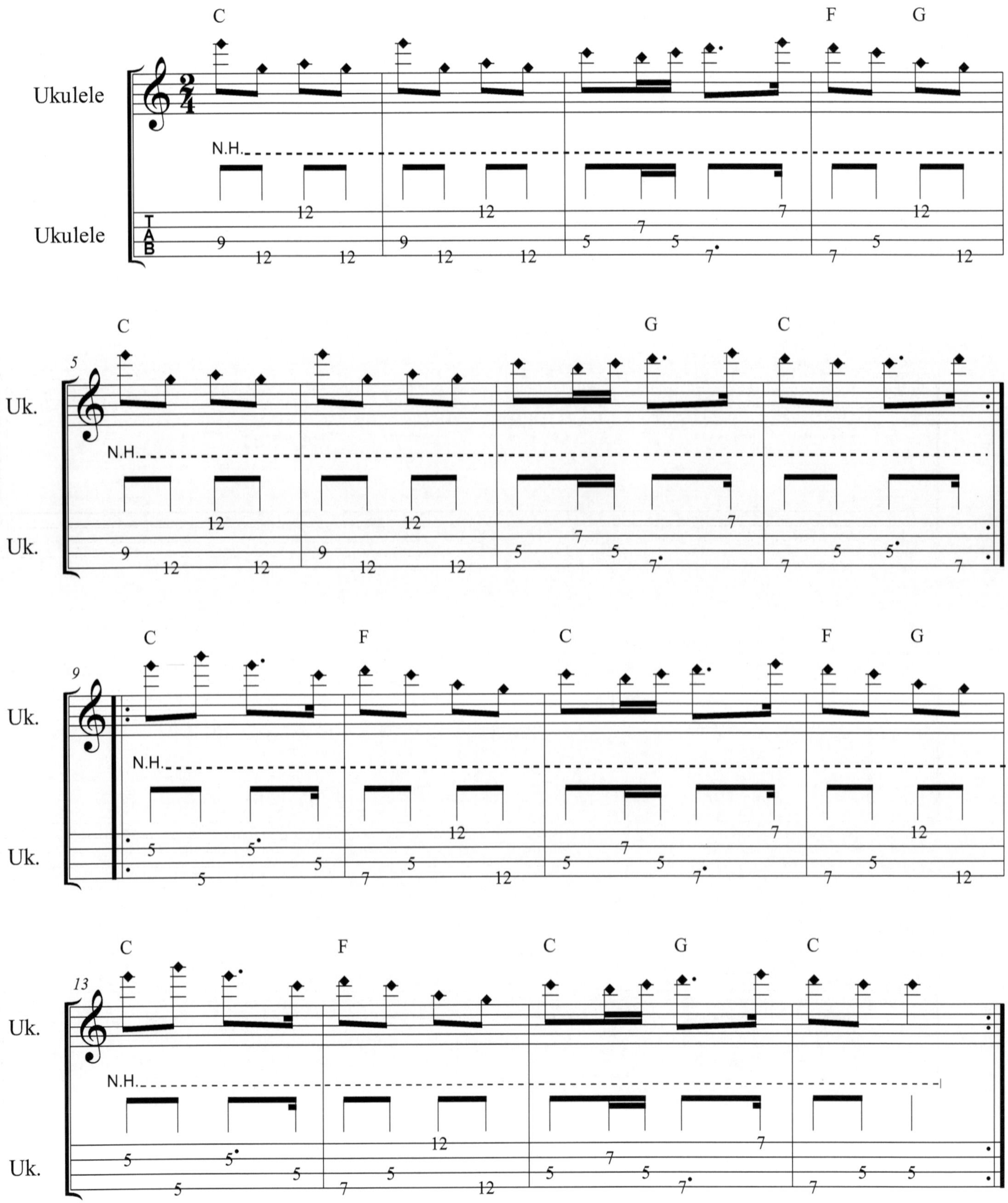

Kesh jig

Score

Irish jig
arr: Ondřej Šárek

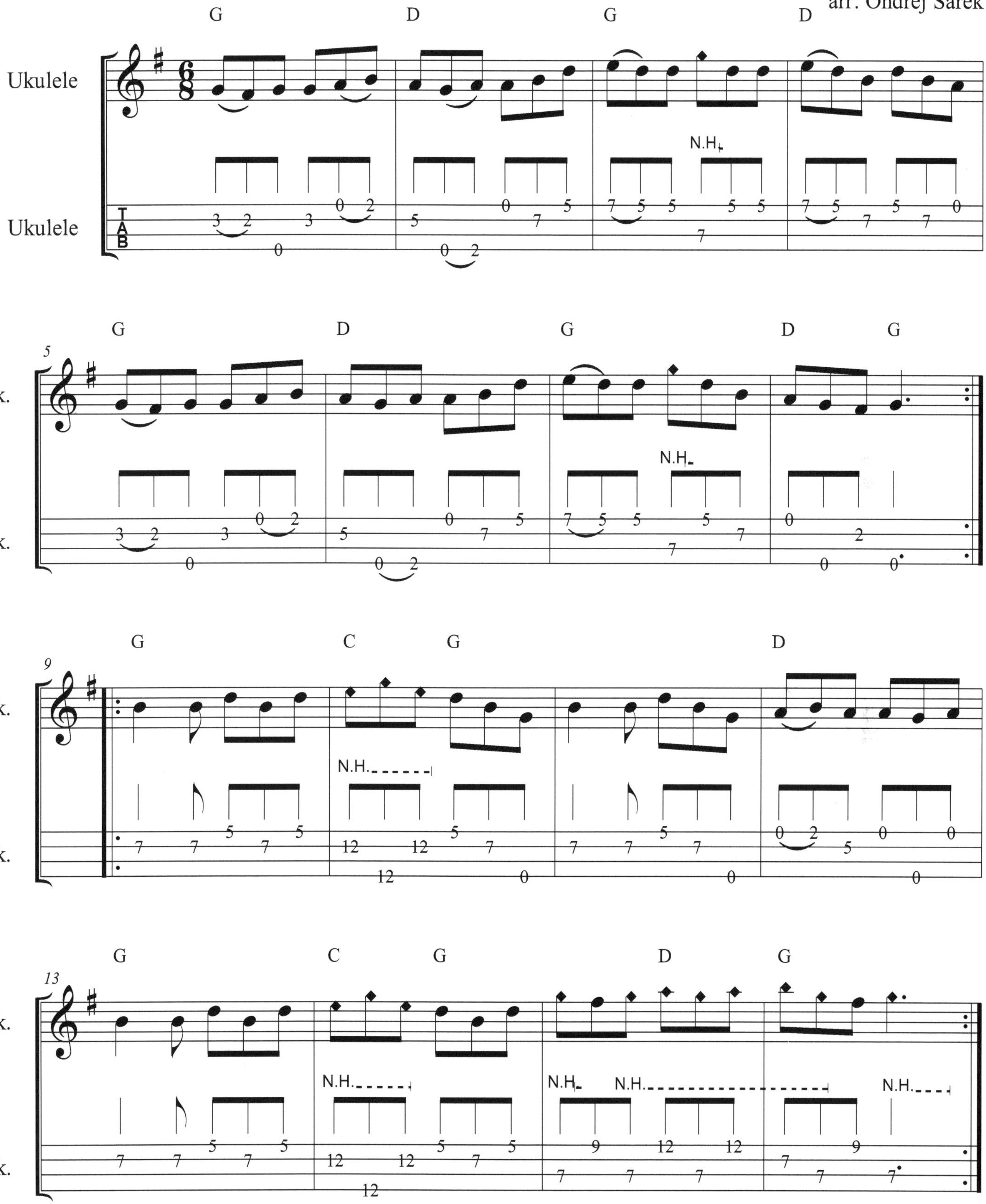

Kum ba yah

Score

Gospel
arr: Ondřej Šárek

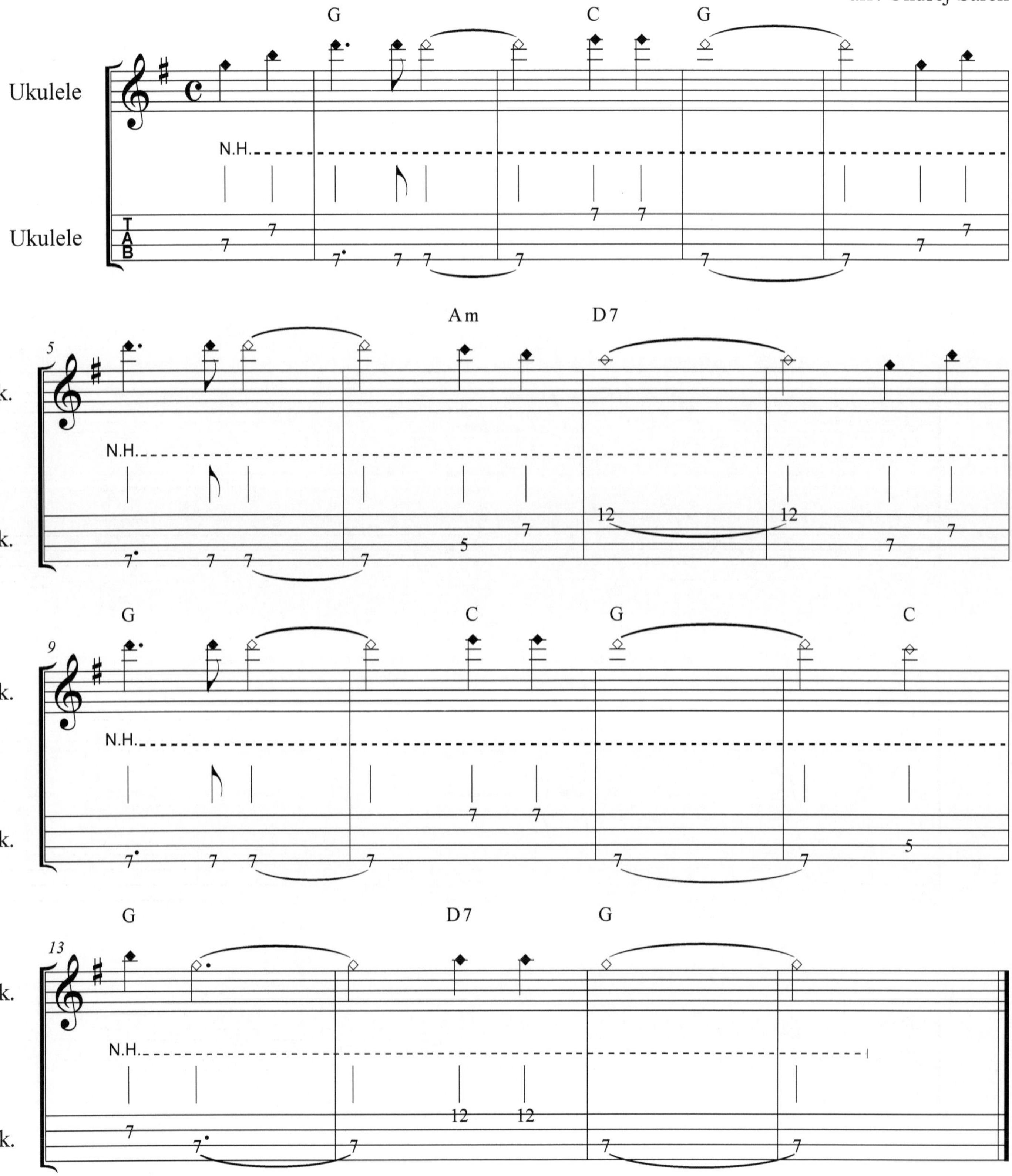

Score

Lassie Wi' The Lint White Locks

Robert Burns
arr: Ondřej Šárek

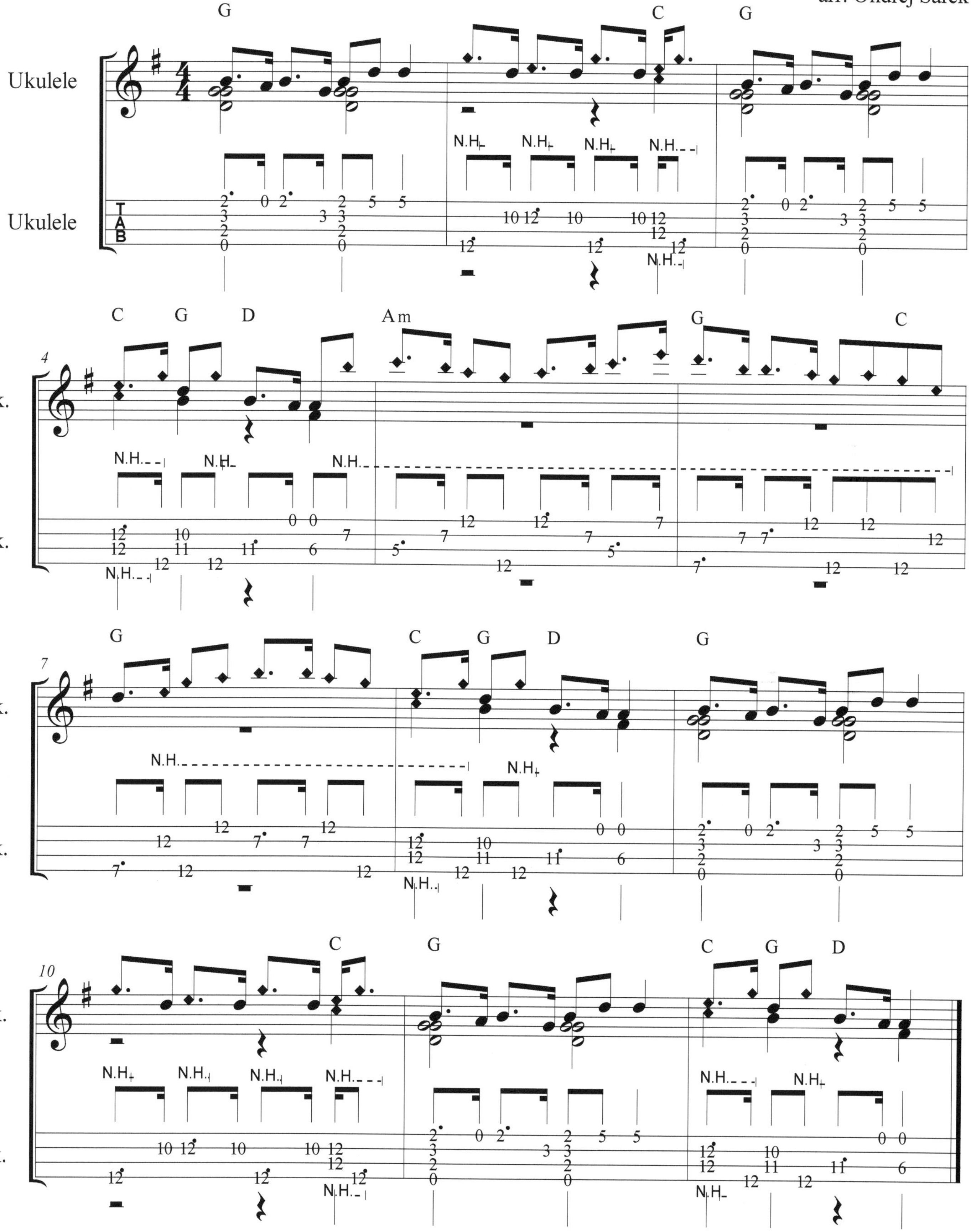

Mary Had A Little Lamb

English folk song
arr: Ondřej Šárek

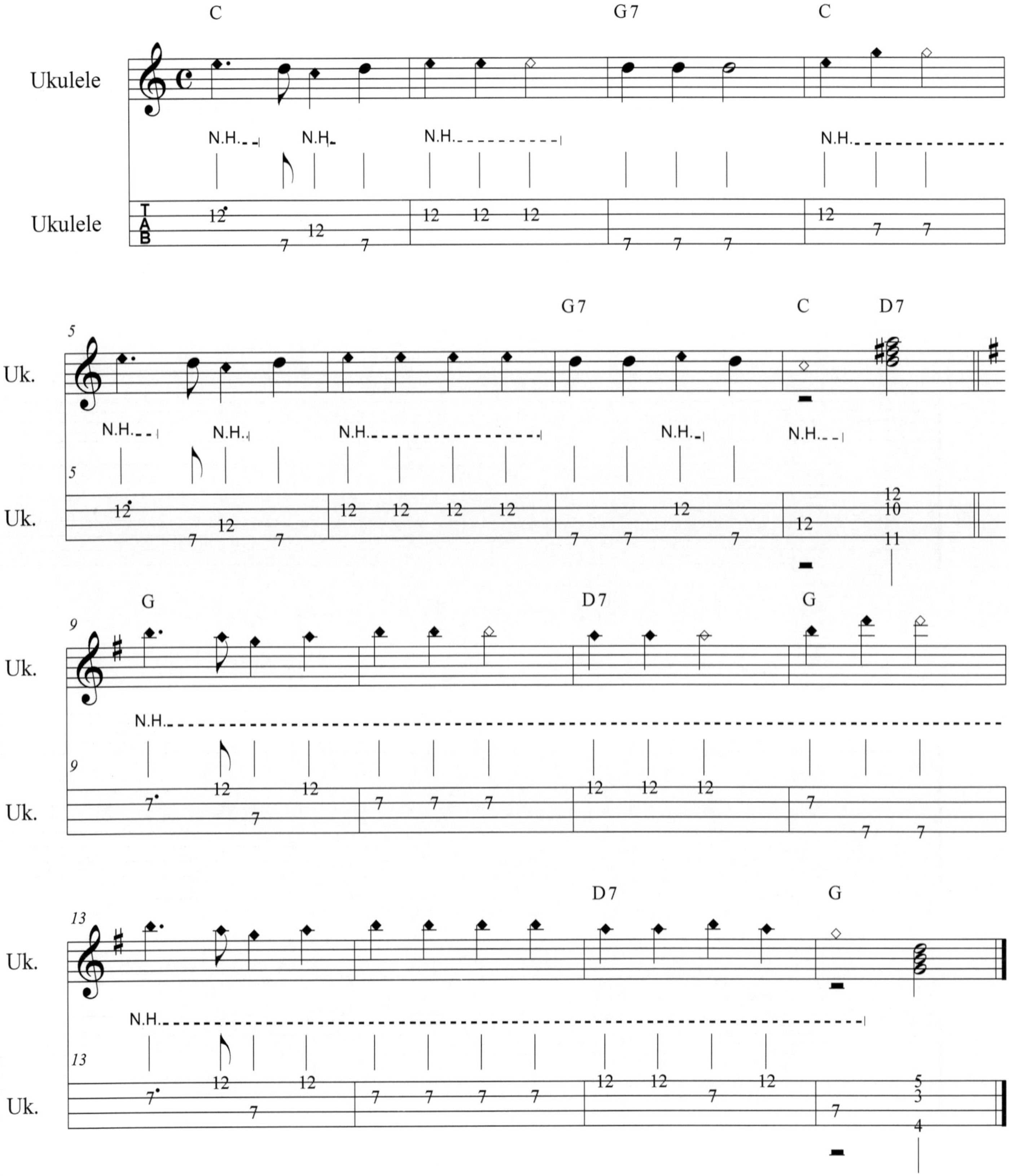

Michael, Row The Boat Ashore

Score

Gospel
arr: Ondřej Šárek

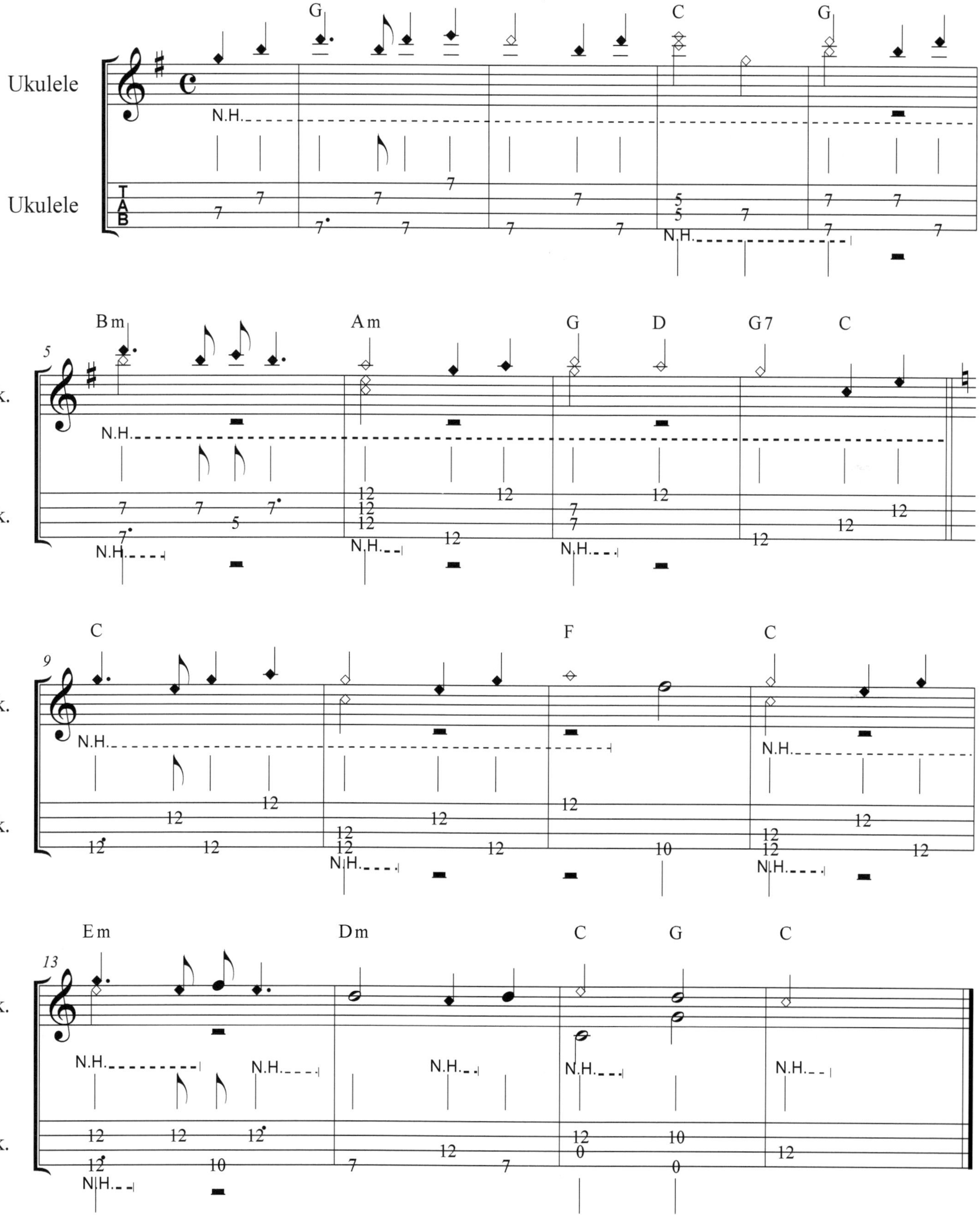

My Love is Like a Red, Red Rose

Score

Robert Burns
arr: Ondřej Šárek

Score

Nearer, My God, to Thee

Lowell Mason
arr: Ondřej Šárek

Score

Non piu andrai

from "Le nozze di Figaro"

(Main Theme)

Wolfgang Amadeus Mozart

arr: Ondřej Šárek

On Top of Old Smokey

Score

American folk song
arr: Ondřej Šárek

Reuben's Train

American folk song
arr: Ondřej Šárek

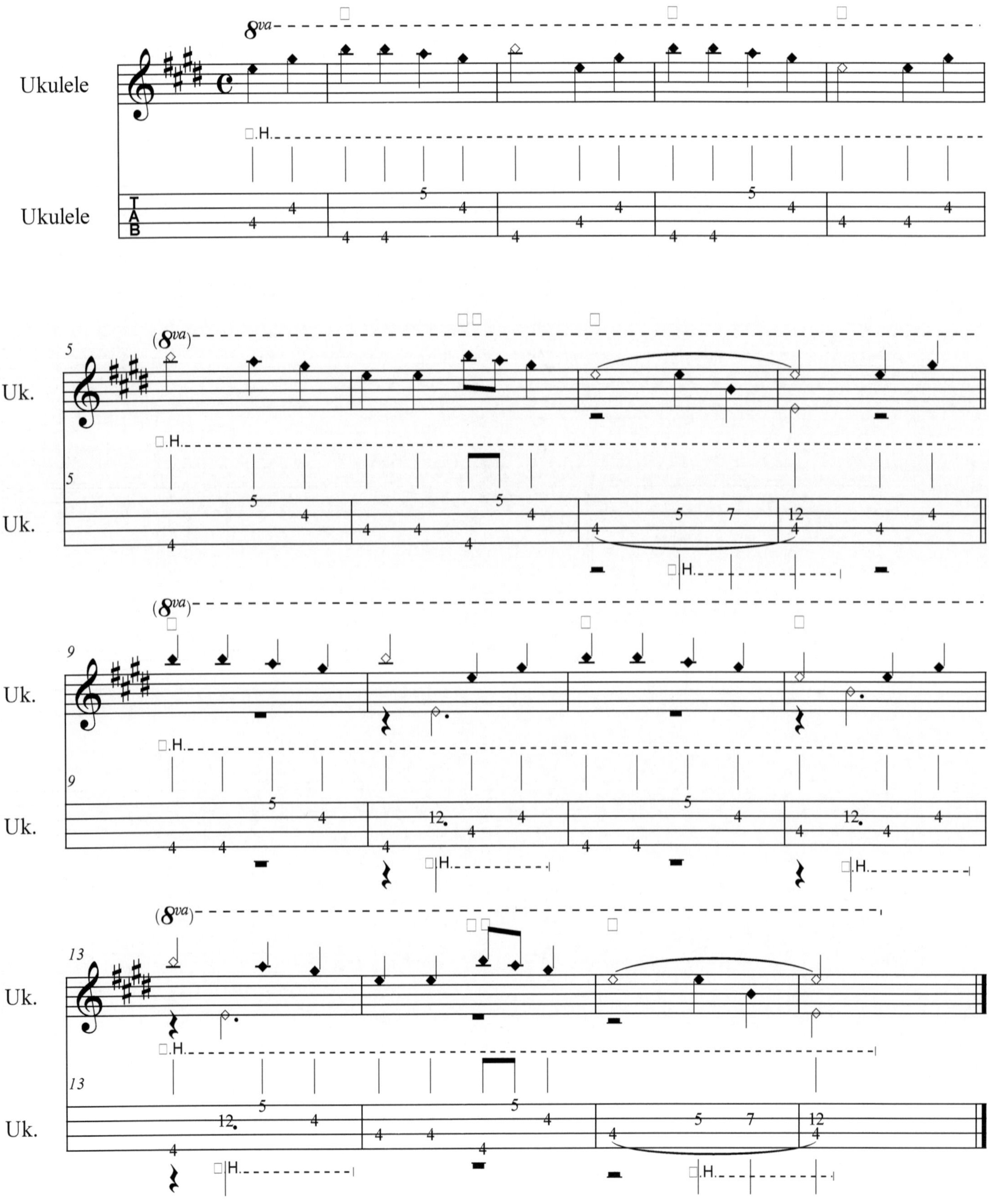

Santa Lucia

Score

Neapolitan folk song
arr: Ondřej Šárek

Silent Night

Franz Xaver Gruber
arr: Ondřej Šárek

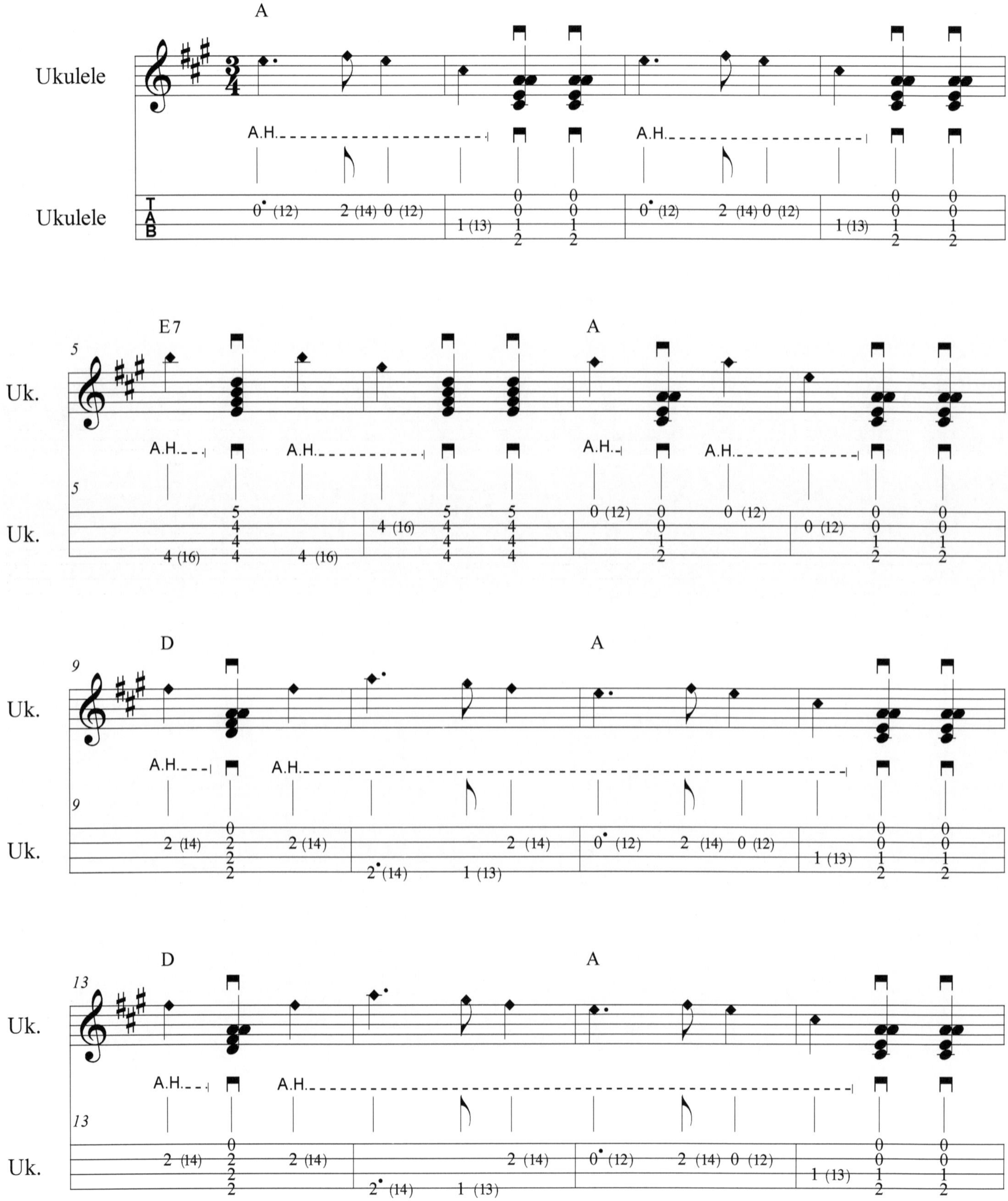

E7
A
Uk.
A.H.
Uk.
E7
A
Uk.
A.H.
Uk.

Shalom Chaverim

Score

Jewish folk song
arr: Ondřej Šárek

Score

St. James Infirmary Blues

American blues song
arr: Ondřej Šárek

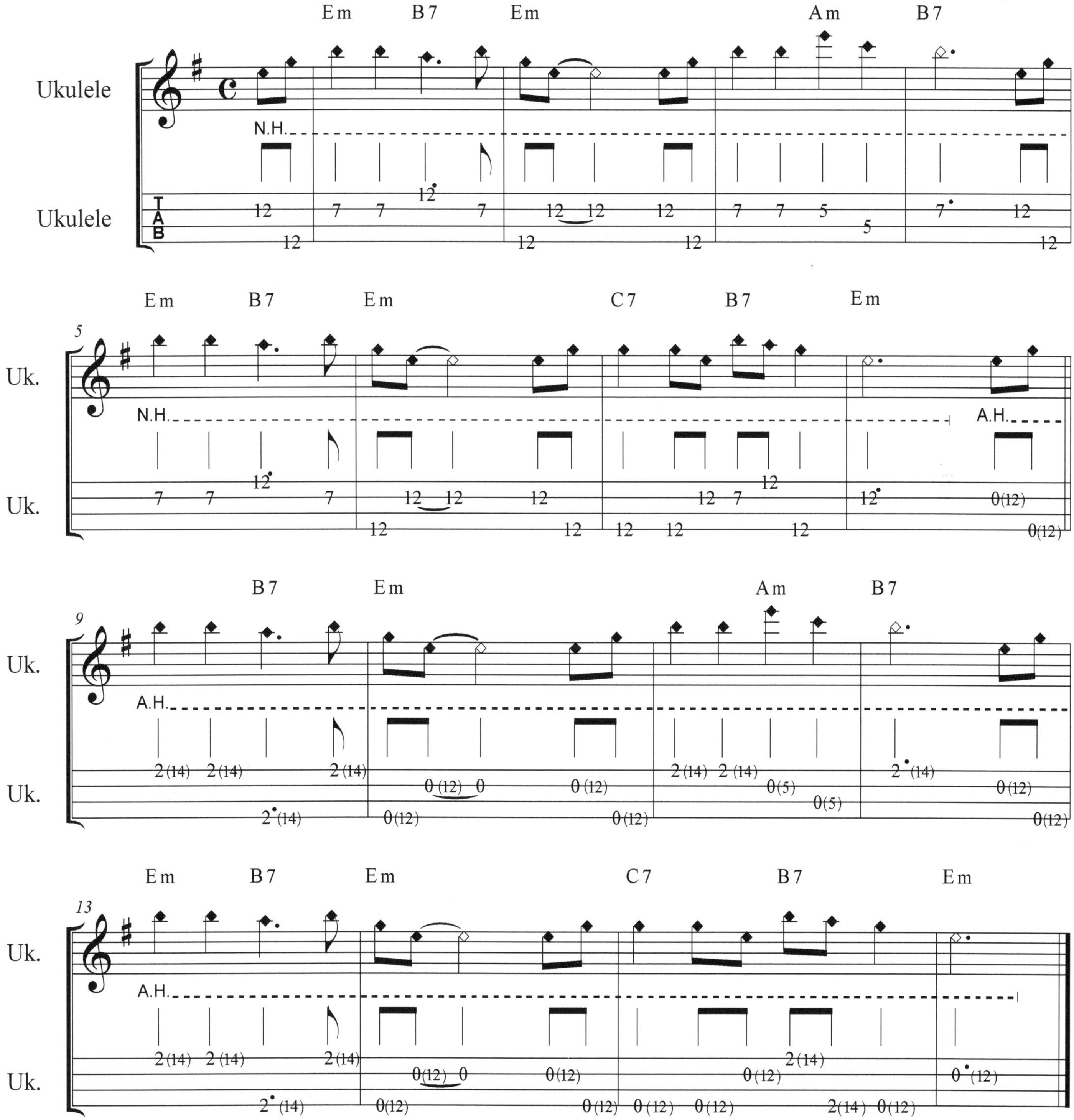

The Streets of Laredo

Score

American folk song
arr: Ondřej Šárek

The Winter It Is Past

Score

Robert Burns
arr: Ondřej Šárek

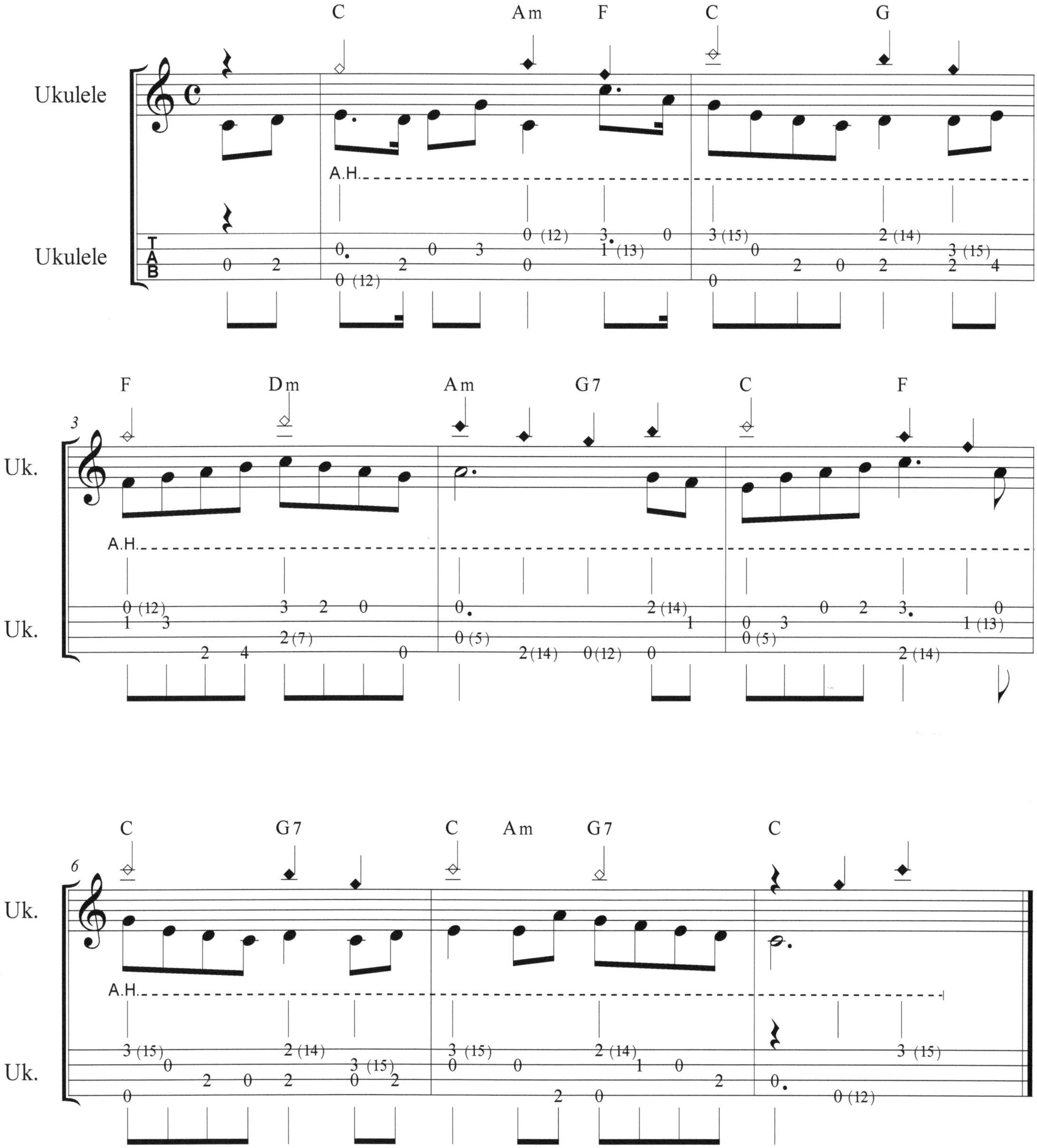

Tum Balalaika

Score

Jewish folk song
arr: Ondřej Šárek

Turkey in the Straw

Score

American folk song
arr: Ondřej Šárek

Swing Low, Sweet Chariot

Score

Gospel
arr: Ondřej Šárek

Vent Frais

Score

French folk song
arr: Ondřej Šárek

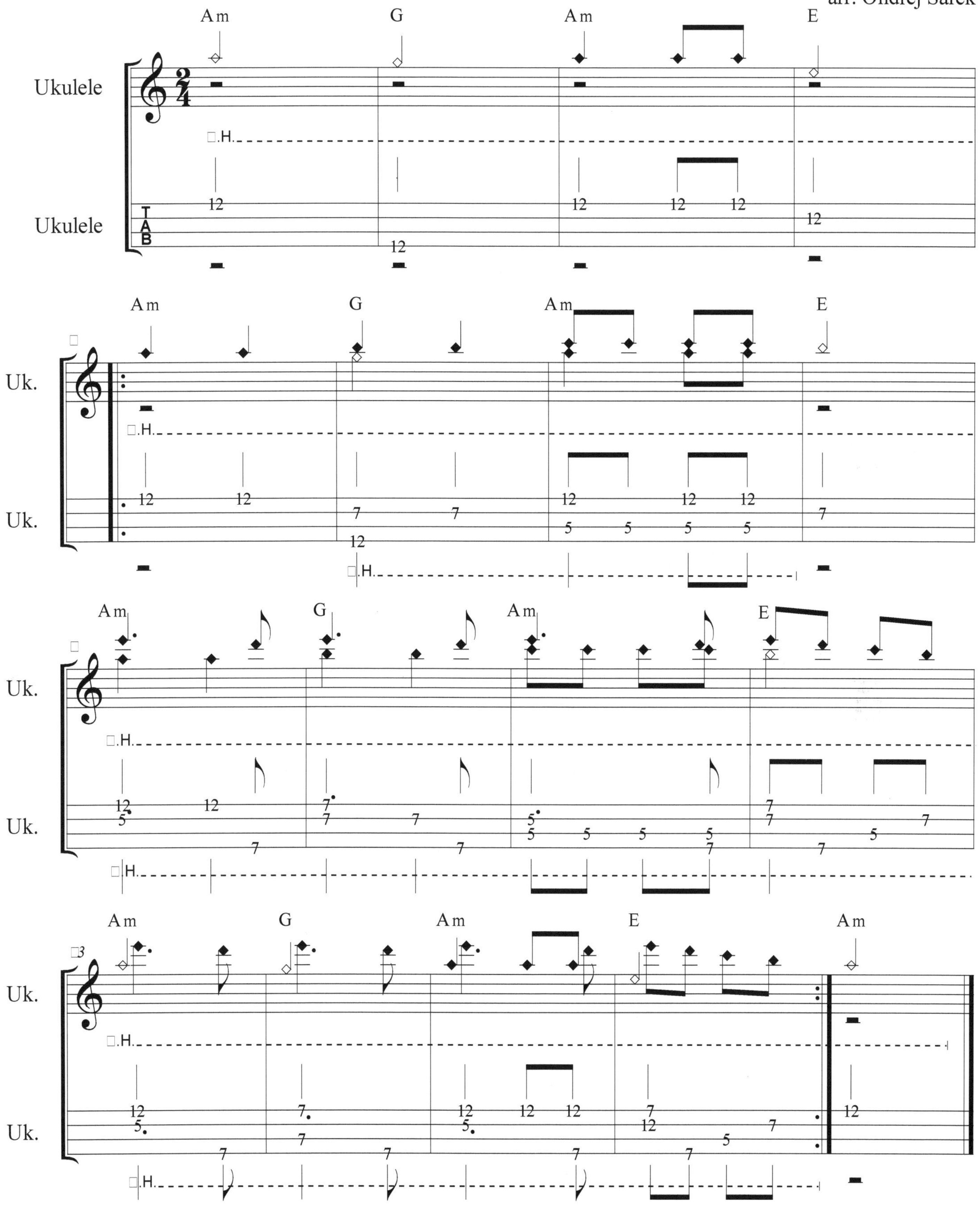

New Ukulele books

For C tuning ukulele

Classics for Ukulele (MB)
Ukulele Bluegrass Solos (MB)
Antonin Dvorak: Biblical Songs (CSI)
Irish tunes for all ukulele (CSI)
Gospel Ukulele Solos (CSI)
Gregorian chant for Ukulele (CSI)
The Czech Lute for Ukulele (CSI)
Romantic Pieces by Frantisek Max Knize for Ukulele (CSI)
Notebook for Anna Magdalena Bach and Ukulele (CSI)
Open Tunings for Ukulel (MB)
Robert Burns songs for ukulele (CSI)
Jewish songs for C tuning ukulele (CSI)
Campanella style songbook for beginner: C tuning ukulele (CSI)
Antonín Dvořák: opera The Jacobin for ukulele ((CSI)
Leopold Mozart's Notebook for Wolfgang Arranged for Ukulele (MB)
The canons for one or two ukuleles (CSI)
Solo and Variations for ukulele *volume 1., 2., 3.* (CSI)
Czech Medieval Ukulele (CSI)
Harmonics for ukulele (CSI)
Christmas Carols for ukulele *volume 1.* (CSI)
Harmonics for ukulele (CSI)

For C tuning with low G

Irish tunes for all ukulele (CSI)
Gospel Ukulele low G Solos(CSI)
Antonin Dvorak: Biblical Songs: for Ukulele with low G (CSI)
Gregorian chant for Ukulele with low G (CSI)
The Czech Lute for Ukulele with low G (CSI)
Romantic Pieces by Frantisek Max Knize for Ukulele with low G (CSI)
Notebook for Anna Magdalena Bach and Ukulele with low G (CSI)
Robert Burns songs for ukulele with low G (CSI)
Jewish songs for ukulele with low G (CSI)
Campanella style songbook for beginner: ukulele with low G (CSI)
Czech Medieval Ukulele with low G (CSI)
Christmas Carols for ukulele with low G *volume 1.* (CSI)

For Baritone ukulele

Irish tunes for all ukulele (CSI)
Gospel Baritone Ukulele Solos (CSI)
Antonin Dvorak: Biblical Songs: for Baritone Ukulele (CSI)
Gregorian chant for Baritone Ukulele (CSI)
The Czech Lute for Baritone Ukulele (CSI)
Romantic Pieces by Frantisek Max Knize for Baritone Ukulele (CSI)
Notebook for Anna Magdalena Bach and Baritone Ukulele (CSI)
Robert Burns songs for Baritone ukulele (CSI)
Jewish songs for baritone ukulele (CSI)
Campanella style songbook for beginner: Baritone ukulele (CSI)
Czech Medieval Baritone Ukulele (CSI)
Christmas Carols for Baritone ukulele *volume 1.* (CSI)

For Baritone ukulele with high D

Jewish songs for baritone ukulele with high D (CSI)
Campanella style songbook for beginner: Baritone ukulele with high D (CSI)
Solo and Variations for Baritone ukulele with high D *volume 1., 2., 3.* (CSI)

For 6 sting ukulele (Lili'u ukulele)

Gospel 6 string Ukulele Solos (CSI)
Gregorian chant for 6 string Ukulele (CSI)
Notebook for Anna Magdalena Bach and 6 string Ukulele (CSI)
Robert Burns songs for 6 string ukulele (CSI)

For Slide ukulele (lap steel ukulele)

Comprehensive Slide Ukulele: Guidance for Slide Ukulele Playing (CSI)
Gospel Slide Ukulele Solos (CSI)
Irish tunes for slide ukulele (CSI)
Robert Burns songs for Slide ukulele (CSI)

For D tuning ukulele

Skola hry na ukulele (G+W s.r.o.)
Irish tunes for all ukulele (CSI)
Jewish songs for D tuning ukulele (CSI)
Campanella style songbook for beginner: D tuning ukulele (CSI)

For EADA tuning ukulele

EADA ukulele tuning (CSI)

Ukulele Duets

Notebook for Anna Magdalena Bach, C tuning ukulele and C tuning ukulele (CSI)
Notebook for Anna Magdalena Bach, C tuning ukulele and Ukulele with low G (CSI)
Notebook for Anna Magdalena Bach, C tuning ukulele and Baritone ukulele (CSI)
Notebook for Anna Magdalena Bach, Ukulele with low G and Ukulele with low G (CSI)
Notebook for Anna Magdalena Bach, Ukulele with low G and Baritone ukulele (CSI)
Notebook for Anna Magdalena Bach, Baritone ukulele and Baritone ukulele (CSI)
The canons for one or two ukuleles (CSI)
Mauro Giuliani arranged for Ukulele Duet (MB)

Guitalele (Guitarlele)

Fingerpicking Guitalele Solo volume I. (CSI)
Fingerpicking Guitalele Solo volume II. (CSI)
Fingerpicking Guitalele Solo volume III. (CSI)
Gregorian chant for Guitalele (CSI)
The Czech Lute for Guitalele (CSI)
Irish tunes for Guitalele (CSI)
The canons for Guitalele (CSI)
Gospel Guitalele Solos (CSI)
Fingerpicking Guitalele Solo volume IV. (CSI)
Fingerpicking Guitalele Solo volume V. - Classical music (CSI)
Czech Medieval Guitalele (CSI)

Cut Capo (Partial Capo) Guitar

Cut capo flatpicking guitar songbook Gospel and Hymns I. (CSI)
Cut capo flatpicking guitar songbook Gospel and Hymns II. (CSI)
Cut capo flatpicking guitar songbook Christmas Carols (CSI)
Cut capo flatpicking guitar songbook Jewish songs (CSI)
Cut capo flatpicking guitar songbook Gregorian chant (CSI)
Cut capo flatpicking guitar songbook Children's Songs (CSI)

DADGAD Guitar

Czech Medieval DADGAD Guitar (CSI)
The canons for DADGAD Guitar (CSI)
Fingerpicking DADGAD Guitar Solo (CSI)
The Czech Lute for DADGAD Guitar (CSI)
Gregorian chant for DADGAD Guitar (CSI)
Gregorian chant for flatpicking DADGAD Guitar (CSI)
Gospel DADGAD Guitar Solos (CSI)
Notebook for Anna Magdalena Bach and DADGAD Guitar (CSI)

EADEAE Guitar

Fingerpicking EADEAE Guitar Solo (CSI)

Mandolin

Czech Medieval Mandolin (CSI)
Gregorian chant for flatpicking Mandolin (CSI)

CGDGCD (Orkney tuning) Guitar

Gospel CGDGCD Guitar Solos (CSI)
Notebook for Anna Magdalena Bach and CGDGCD Guitar (CSI)
Gregorian chant for flatpicking CGDGCD Guitar (CSI)
Fingerpicking CGDGCD Guitar Solo (CSI)

EADGBE Guitar

Czech Medieval EADGBE Guitar (CSI)
Gregorian chant for flatpicking EADGBE Guitar (CSI)
The canons for EADGBE Guitar (CSI)
The Czech Lute for EADGBE Guitar (CSI)

DADGBD (Double drop D tuning) Guitar

Gospel Double drop D tuning Guitar Solos (CSI)
Notebook for Anna Magdalena Bach and Double drop D tuning Guitar (CSI)

New Anglo Concertina books

For C/G 30-button Wheatstone Lachenal System

Gospel Anglo Concertina Solos (CSI)
Notebook for Anna Magdalena Bach and Anglo Concertina (CSI)
Robert Burns songs for Anglo Concertina (CSI)
The Czech Lute for Anglo Concertina (CSI)
Gregorian chant for Anglo Concertina (CSI)

For C/G 20-button

Gospel C/G Anglo Concertina Solos (CSI)
Robert Burns songs for C/G Anglo Concertina (CSI)
Gregorian chant for Anglo Concertina (CSI)

New Diatonic Accordion (Melodeon) books

For G/C diatonic accordion

Bass songbook for G/C melodeon (CSI)
Cross row style songbook for beginner G/C diatonic accordion (CSI)
Gospel G/C diatonic accordion Solos (CSI)

For C/F diatonic accordion

Cross row style songbook for beginner C/F diatonic accordion (CSI)
Gospel C/F diatonic accordion Solos (CSI)

For D/G diatonic accordion

Cross row style songbook for beginner D/G diatonic accordion (CSI)
Gospel D/G diatonic accordion Solos (CSI)

Publishing House

CSI = CreateSpace Independent Publishing Platform
MB = Mel Bay Publications
G+W = G+W s.r.o.

11511856R00038

Printed in Great Britain
by Amazon.co.uk, Ltd.,
Marston Gate.